the GOD WHO *puts us* BACK TOGETHER

the GOD WHO *puts us* BACK TOGETHER

Gene Shelburne

COLLEGE PRESS
PUBLISHING COMPANY
Joplin, Missouri

Although the events are real, the names and other details in
some of these stories have been changed for the purpose of
protecting the people depicted and/or their families.

Library of Congress Cataloging-in-Publication Data

Shelburne, Gene, 1939–
    The God who puts us back together/Gene Shelburne.
        p. cm.
    ISBN 0-89900-744-9 (pbk.)
    1. Suffering—Religious aspects—Christianity—Case
studies. 2. Christian biography—United States I. Title.
BT732.7.S525 1995
248.8'6—dc20   95-37965
                                                                       CIP

Contents

of it? Can we speak to homosexuals so that they hear Christ's welcoming, constraining grace?

Introduction

"After you have suffered a little while, the God of all grace. . .will himself restore you" (1 Peter 5:10).

Our world is full of broken people. People whose dreams have been shattered by divorce and bankruptcy and addictions. People whose families have fallen apart because of anger and greed and immaturity. People whose hearts have been crushed by deceit and hatefulness and cruelty.

When life unravels for celebrities, their fiascoes make headlines. When Michael Milken goes to jail, when Donald Trump gets a high-dollar divorce, when Magic Johnson tells the world he has AIDS, when Woody Allen gets tagged for sexual abuse, everybody knows it. Their messes provide grist for public gossip. Nobody seems to see or care about their tears.

But for every public debacle like these you could

uncover tens of thousands of equally devastating disasters causing just as much heartache for little people whose names most of us will never know.

In my own small circle the tales of human brokenness defy belief. Close friends called one night to tell us in tears that their only daughter, away at college, had taken her life. Last year a teacher friend suddenly lost the sight of one eye. Now her terror grows because the other one seems to be failing. A Christian veterinarian and his wife weep as they tell us about an ex-daughter-in-law who refuses to let them visit the grandchildren they adore. While another dear couple give up the peace of their fifties and sixties to raise the grandson their skirt-chasing, drug-using son abandoned.

Just among my own acquaintances the catalog of disrupted, broken lives seems endless. In today's turbulent society, your list is probably just as long. I can tell you about one precious little girl who grew up in our church. By the time she was fourteen she had syphilis. By the time she was nineteen she had been through two husbands. Since that time she and her live-in lover have fed her three urchins and paid their light bill by begging from local churches.

Or I might let you visit with the mother who first cut herself off from her entire family by defending the lifestyle of her two homosexual sons, and then threatened her own sanity by helping both of them end their AIDS agony by suicide. Brokenness. That's what I'm talking about.

Are more people broken today than ever before? Or do we think so just because this is the age we live in?

All around me lives are disintegrating. If you look at the word *integrity*, you can easily see that *disintegration* is the lack of it. Right? That explains much of the moral brokenness we see around us. Men and women lacking basic moral values make choices that are sure to wreck their lives. But that's only one part of the brokenness in our world. How do you explain the hearts and lives that are decimated by sudden unemployment, by unexpected disability, by mental illness, by death?

Ever since the day when they put up the "Posted" signs in the Garden of Eden, men and women have been trying to figure out why our world is bent and broken. My purpose is not to explain why, but to proclaim the Good News that our condition is not permanent, because we worship a God who delights in putting broken people back together again.

"After you have suffered a little while," the Scriptures promise, "the God of all grace will himself *restore* you." He will make you well. He will make you whole.

The old fisherman, Peter, understood the word he chose here to describe God's goodness. It was a term his comrades used to describe how their torn and damaged nets were cleaned and mended and folded for future use. Because the fishermen valued their nets, at the end of each day they were "restored."

The apostle Paul used the same word in Galatians 6:1 to tell us to *restore* sinful saints with a spirit of gentleness. Do you suppose he had heard the word on the lips of his physician friend Luke? It was a word a doctor might use to describe setting a broken bone. With his tender healing skills, the physician "restored" the fractured limb, making it well and whole again.

I love this biblical picture of the Lord. After we have suffered, he brings grace to mend our brokenness. He puts us back together again.

Like Humpty Dumpty, some of us have fallen hard and shattered ourselves into more pieces than we could ever hope to have reassembled. With man it would be impossible. But for the God who created light out of darkness, for the God who summoned life out of a tomb, for this God restoration is not only possible. It is promised.

With two possible exceptions. First, God will not overrule our moral choices. At the heart of the gospel is our freedom to choose — even when our choices are wrong and ruinous. If we choose to stay broken, God will honor our decision, even if it breaks his heart. In cases like this God's grace can still be seen as he heals the broken hearts of family members and friends who are devastated by our sinful ways. At least two of the episodes in this book will reflect situations like this.

A second exception may be diseases, disabilities, or physical damage that cannot be medically repaired. God does not promise any of us perfect health, but he does promise to be near to us in troubled times and to strengthen our spirits when our bodies fail. He will give us "grace to help in time of need."

My father-in-law was a journeyman carpenter whose wide range of skills included furniture repair. He was a believer in Wilhold Glue. With his clamps and his trusty glue bottle, he would confidently tackle the task of mending broken chair rungs and bedposts. To any curious observer he always repeated the advertising slogan of the Wilhold Glue manufacturers. "When I put it back together with this glue," he smilingly boasted, "it will be stronger than when it was new."

So it can be for our broken lives when the God of all grace puts us back together again.

Miz Murphy:
Tougher Than Death

"O death, where is thy sting?" (1 Corinthians 15:55).

The first girl I ever fell in love with was Martha Murphy.

Martha was a cheerleader at Tivy High School. I was in fifth grade.

Martha lived catty-corner across the street from me. Until that fateful fifth-grade year when she broke my heart, she was just "the girl across the street." I saw her coming and going every day with school friends. I doubt that she even knew I existed.

But . . . I'm getting ahead of my story.

Back in the summer of 1946 when my family moved to Kerrville, Texas, we built a brand new house on Clay Street. The Murphys' big old frame house was the only home on the other side of the street. It looked like it had been there forever.

Like so many of the turn-of-the-century houses, it had a spacious porch across much of the front and down one side, with white bannisters all around it. And with a porch swing, of course. In its day the house had been elegant. A real show place, probably. With rooms upstairs in the attic and more room in a basement below, the Murphys' home was not a small house.

It was painted banana-pudding yellow. By the time we moved there the paint was beginning to peel. Disrepair was peeking out of every crevice. The place needed a man. Martha would have been twelve or thirteen then, I guess. She lived in that huge house alone with her mother, whom the neighborhood kids called Miz Murphy.

Miz Murphy was an older lady than you might suspect from the age of her daughter. When I tell you how old she was, remember that I was only seven or eight at the time and everybody over twenty looks like they're a hundred to a kid that age. But Miz Murphy did have an "old" look about her. She wore her graying hair in a bun on the back of her head like my grandmas did. And I never saw her without her granny apron on. She might have been fifty but I guess her nearer to sixty when we first met her.

In the early hours on summer days before the south Texas sun got too hot, we would see Miz Murphy puttering around in the big garden behind the house. The rest of the day she stayed busy inside. Canning food. Cooking continually. Sewing and washing and cleaning and ironing. Miz Murphy was seldom idle. She had too much pluck to sit around and mope.

But if she had wanted to, she had plenty of reasons to mope.

Mr. Murphy died before we came onto the scene. I never knew much about him. I could only infer his presence, much like we deduce that God created the world because we can see what all He made and how well He made it. The handiwork of the late Mr. Murphy was still evident on many corners of their property. His absence was also apparent in all the things that needed to be propped up or torn down or put back together again.

It never occurred to me when I was seven or eight to wonder what kind of man he had been. Or to wonder how Miz Murphy felt about his being gone. Looking back, I realize now that burying her husband and coping with such a loss had prepared Miz Murphy for the terrible times that lay in store for her.

By the time it was all over Miz Murphy had a graduate degree in losing what we love.

My Boy Bill

We had been neighbors to Miz Murphy for at least a couple of years before we found out that she had a son named Bill.

"I guess we're going to have to look around and find a used bicycle for Gene," Mom remarked off the cuff one day to Miz Murphy. I was selling *Grit* newspapers on Fridays and Saturdays from one end of the town to the other. On foot. A bicycle would double the territory I could cover.

"I've got my son's old bicycle in the garage," Miz Murphy volunteered. "He'll never use it again. Why don't I just sell it to you?"

A rickety old garage stood behind the house on the north-side property line. Probably built for a Model T.

Miz Murphy tugged open one of the sagging doors and together we dug through head-high piles of past treasures until we unearthed a dust-covered red bicycle. 1930 vintage. Tires rotten. Bearings squeaky dry. But a solid old bicycle. In better shape than its original owner.

Bill rode that bicycle when he was in high school. Before he left home to fight in the Big war. Before he came home from the German front to spend his days in a V.A. mental hospital. Shell-shock, they called it back then. Post-Vietnam syndrome, we called it 30 years later.

Bill Murphy lived in his own private hell of tears and terror. He awoke screaming from dreams. When he was like that he was dangerous. To his mother. To Martha. Bill was a big man with massive biceps. In the odd moments when his mind was clear, he was a gentle, loving fellow. But when the spirits of military mayhem raged in his soul, he was a violent, dangerous man who could wipe out anything or anybody who got in his way without knowing what damage he had done.

One spring day in 1948 Bill came home. Doctors at the hospital decided he was handling his problems well enough to return to his mother's house. Looking back, I'm sure our block must have buzzed as the adults up and down the street held whispered consultations about possible dangers Bill posed to themselves and their offspring. But everybody behaved and, despite any fears or reservations we had about his presence, we welcomed Bill back to the little chunk of real estate where he had grown up before the war ruined him.

If Bill really was dangerous (and he probably was), he did nothing to allay the jitters of the mothers nearby when he decided to take out the huge mulberry tree which had grown up against the west wall of his mother's house. That was my introduction to Bill. I came home from school one afternoon and found our street half blocked by the limbs of the towering tree he had expertly felled. The limbs of the fallen giant filled the Murphys' large front yard and extended part way into the narrow street between our houses.

Bill spent most of every day for the next two weeks hacking that monster into firewood, deftly plying a razor sharp axe. Before and after school hours he had a spellbound audience of half a dozen little boys, who watched goggled eyed as his muscular arms swung the heavy tool like a toy, spraying wood chips in every direction. This newfound Paul Bunyan became a Pied Piper, entrancing all the small fry on our block.

Knowing little about Bill's war-related problems, it never occurred to us kids to wonder if his mother was glad to have her son home again. Or if she lay awake at night wondering what would happen to her and Martha if Bill woke up fighting Germans in the dark. Whether Miz Murphy feared him or not, Bill's troubles must have recurred. His visit home lasted barely three weeks. Just long enough for the firewood to be corded and the wood chips to be raked up. As suddenly as Bill came, he vanished. Like the tree he cut down, one day he was there; the next he was gone. Back to the psycho ward of a Veterans Hospital somewhere downstate. I never saw Bill Murphy again.

Things on our block got quiet again, and Miz Murphy returned to her normal round of chores. What a mixture of emotions must have torn at the heart of that mother! For the space of an entire World War she had prayed daily for her son to come home. And when he got there, he was a stranger who frightened her by his moody silence and by the demented look in his eyes. After spending a week being terrified by her own boy, Miz Murphy surely began praying again. Praying that the son she loved so much could go back to the lock-up ward. Back where his berserk behavior could be controlled. Before it caused a tragedy worse than the one she was already grieving about. When they came to take Bill away, can you imagine the conflicting torrents of relief and remorse which swept through that poor mother's soul?

Without any audible complaints, Miz Murphy set about restoring a normal, stable life for herself and Martha. They had given up the only two men who could have improved their lot. One to death. The other to a fate worse than death. Any happiness or hope to brighten their days these two women would have to provide for each other.

Martha, Martha

That fall was the fateful time when my heart was smitten by Martha Murphy.

Football season came to our little town with a fever-pitch of excitement that year. Our little school was playing up two divisions. Like David, we were tweaking the beak of some big-city Goliaths and relishing every surprising victory. Martha was a cheerleader that year, so she was right in the middle of the fanfare and hoopla that swept the town. When it looked like our tiny district had a bonafide shot at the big-school state championship, the football craziness oozed across the street that divided the high school from the elementary campus. School officials began to turn loose the fourth, fifth, and sixth graders to join the frenzy of the afternoon pep rallies every Friday. That's where I first realized that "the girl across the street" was a dazzling, dimpled, heart-throbbing beauty. At one of the first pep rallies she actually smiled at me and said hello. Back in those days we didn't know anything about atomic reactors, but I assure you that I suffered meltdown right there on the spot. From that Friday on, just a glimpse of Martha Murphy was enough to transport me to the seventh heaven.

Then came the news.

"Martha's sick," Miz Murphy told my mom. "Bad flu, I guess." But the belly pains became more intense that night, so Miz Murphy summoned the family doctor.

"Let's get her to the hospital," he urged after his examination. "I'm pretty sure we're dealing with a hot appendix."

Back then an appendectomy was still major surgery. Without doubt its long aftermath would knock Martha out of the festivities of that fabulous football year. But in the days before antibiotics the danger of waiting was too great. Reluctantly, Miz Murphy nodded O.K. to the doc.

My first hint of just how serious things were was the appearance of the town's ancient ambulance. On our street, no less. Backed up to Miz Murphy's front door. I watched, speechless, as they loaded the stretcher bearing Martha's petite frame, and slowly drove away.

I don't know when we first heard the bad news. That night late. Or early the next day. Before long everybody on the block knew the doctor had been wrong. Pretty precious Martha did not have appendicitis.

Inside her abdomen the surgeons had found cancer. Lots of it. Widespread. They sewed her up and sent her home in a few days. To die.

Martha didn't last long. But those days of her dying were awful days for me. Most of the town went right on chasing its football fantasy. Somber tributes were paid to Martha at a pep rally or two, but most of the town's inhabitants were not touched by Martha's dying like we were. They didn't live across the street from her house. They didn't see church friends and school chums coming and going in a constant procession through the Murphy's front door. They didn't see the agony that etched itself more deeply each day on Miz Murphy's face. And they didn't love Martha. Not like I did.

Martha was my first love. She was also my first encounter with the capricious cruelty of death. "It is appointed for all men to die," the Scriptures assure us. But that's for old folks, I thought. That's for people who are weary and worn out. Not for lively young ladies with all the sweetness and fruitfulness of life yet within them. My ten-year-old assessment of the situation was not far off base. Back when the skies above L.A. were still clean and clear, the incredible inappropriateness of Martha's dying brooded over our neighborhood like a pall of untimely smog. Young and old alike simply could not believe what was happening.

Martha's funeral was one of the biggest our little town had ever known. The high school turned out, and neighbors clustered in the church to say goodbye to that sweet child who had been the apple of everybody's eye. When all the Scriptures were read and the eulogies were spoken and the hymns were sung, the crowd dispersed to return to their normal duties. Just like folks at funerals always do. And Miz Murphy went home. Back to her big old house. Alone.

Life After Martha

Have you noticed how calloused and indifferent life can be toward the dead? For three or four days, perhaps a week at most, we pause when death comes near. We close our stores, we take off work, we skip school. Life stops. While we bury the dead.

Then the relatives all fly home. The neighbors all go back to work. The preacher goes back to the church to work on next Sunday's sermon. And the flow of life around us quickly resumes its normal pace as if nothing had ever slowed down. In a very few days everybody seems to have forgotten. Everybody, that is, except the widow whose loneliness seems to deepen with each passing day. Everybody except the mother, who still can't bear to enter the missing child's room. Everybody except Miz Murphy, to whom Martha had been her reason for each day's rising, her motive for each day's labor, her occasion for each day's laughter. Soon my own childish interests turned to other things. I forgot all about Martha. And, as I look back today, it amazes me that in those days following the funeral I cannot remember ever wondering how Miz Murphy was making it. How she was managing to face each day without the one who had been the only ray of light left in a life that had already known more than its share of grief and loss. How in heaven's name did that poor soul stay in that cavernous house all by herself? Eating alone. Sleeping alone. Weeping alone.

One widow wrote:

"She lives alone," I heard him say
Who sadly cast a glance my way.
"It must be hard, when day is done,
To set the table just for one.
What does she do when twilight falls,
All alone within those walls?"
                    (Grace E. Easley)

Perhaps I did not wonder about such things back then because Miz Murphy resumed her own routines almost as if nothing had happened. At the ripe old age of ten I had no way to know just how wise this grief-stricken lady was. She had every reason to hole up in her house, cursing God for her accumulated miseries and surrendering what was left of her days to depression and despair. Like ancient Jacob, who mourned for his favorite wife and then for his favorite son, Miz Murphy could have moaned, "I will go to my grave in tears." Who would have blamed her if she had simply given up? But she didn't.

Martha was gone, but the garden still would need planting. Martha was gone, but the bread still needed baking. Martha was gone, and Bill was gone, and Mr. Murphy was gone, but life still needed living. Miz Murphy seemed to subscribe to the sentiments of the psalmist who said, "Weeping may tarry for the night, but joy comes with the morning" (Psalm 30:5).

If not this morning, then some morning.

Soon.

If I can keep going and don't let grief dictate the continual focus of my actions and my thoughts.

Unlike some of my good friends, Miz Murphy refused to let the death of her dearest ones mark the end of her own life. With resilient faith and fortitude she resolved to keep on living. As a gangly kid I was wowed by the strength of Bill Murphy's muscles. As a man I know now that the real strength in that home belonged to his gray-haired mother.

Death, Where Is Thy Sting?

"Upon this rock I will build my church," Jesus announced. And then he promised, "The powers of death shall not prevail against it" (Matthew 16:18). Because He lives in us, we do not have to be overcome by death. In Jesus we are greater than grief. To surrender to sorrow is to ignore our Lord and to deny the power of his resurrection. Of course we weep when our loved ones die. Just as our Lord shed tears beside the crypt of Lazarus. Of course our hearts break when children and parents or long-time mates are wrenched apart by Satan's nastiest scheme. But Miz Murphy reminds us that we can come out winners in the battle with death.

George MacDonald is surely right when he says that "past tears are present strength." Having once survived the ravages of grief, we know that the Lord does indeed provide "grace to help in time of need." Having put our head and our hearts back together again when death battered and broke us, we now know that sorrow is not forever. When grief swept over his life, the German poet Heine wrote:

> *First, I thought, almost despairing,*
> *This must crush my spirit now;*
> *Yet I bore it, and am bearing —*
> *Only do not ask me how.*

Looking back at such times from a distance, however, we do begin to know how we survived. We know that we got up and got out among friends. Even when we didn't feel like it. We know that we kept on seeking God's strength in worship. Even when it seemed like He was not there. We know that we conquered sorrow by affirming the goodness of life that remained. Looking back, we know that the brightest moments in those dark days of the soul were the times when we stirred ourselves to do some small act of kindness for someone else whose heart was aching. Today we know we came through those grief-shrouded days by doggedly attending to our most obvious duties, accepting simple drudgery when creativity and enthusiasm had fled. In his touching book, *A Severe Mercy*, Sheldon Vanauken tells the tale of his wild grief after he lost his young wife. "The disappearance of the grief is not followed by happiness," Vanauken says. "It is followed by emptiness." Most of us who have covered a grave have known that emptiness. And we have experienced the slow emergence of God's goodness, filling our hearts with new interests and teaching us how to love again.

Miz Murphy never talked to me about stuff like this. She just lived it. In such a sturdy way that even a kid like me could not miss what he was seeing. I doubt that she had ever read the poet who screamed, "Death, do not be proud!", but she embodied his cry. Like our Lord facing the cross, she looked death squarely in the face without flinching. Satan knew when he got through with Miz Murphy that he had met his match. Just like he lost that day on Calvary. Just like he loses every time you and I come through grief with our faith intact and our hope enhanced. Jesus soundly whipped the devil on Golgotha, and the Scriptures proclaim that "He always leads us in triumph" (2 Corinthians 2:14). You need to hear those words if you are wrestling with recent sorrow. "He *always* leads us in triumph." But that means, of course, we have to let *Him* lead.

✳ ✳ ✳ ✳ ✳

Only a few years after Martha Murphy died, our family moved away. But we returned one summer for a week, and my folks rented two or three rooms in Miz Murphy's fine old house. Martha had been gone then for at least five years. Years that had accentuated the "oldness" of her mother. Miz Murphy's hair was now silvery white. She was skinnier than I remembered, like older ladies often are. She had given up gardening the year before. But it seemed to me as we visited with her that week that any strength her body had given up had been absorbed by her spirit. She was living evidence of Paul's words, "Though our outer nature is wasting away, our inner nature is being renewed every day" (2 Corinthians 4:16). Which seems all the more remarkable, considering the traumas of grief and loss Miz Murphy had endured. Out of her brokenness God had brought forth saintly wholeness. In her later days she was truly a radiant, happy person. With the Christians of all ages, she had learned to say, "O grave, where is your victory? O death, where is your sting?"

Death had done its worst to Miz Murphy, and she was still smiling.

God's Hit Man

"He who says he is in the light and hates his brother is in the darkness still" (1 John 2:9).

For obvious reasons the names in the tale I'm about to tell you have been changed, but the story is true. It is a parable of hope and healing for victims of pulpit abuse.

Lt. Glenn Smith was a deputy sheriff for Maricopa County, the large county that covers the central part of Arizona including the metropolitan area of Phoenix. Lt. Smith was everything you might hope for a lawman to be. A big, gentle, easy-going fellow who liked people. When it came to little kids or to people in trouble, he had a heart as big as the desert he patrolled.

So when they finally unraveled the bizarre events of that fateful day it came as no surprise to anybody who knew him that this exemplary sheriff evidently had stopped to assist what he thought was a farm worker in a dinged-up old pickup that appeared to be broken down. He pulled his patrol car in behind the pickup, which was parked in the shade of a cottonwood tree beside an irrigation ditch, and he got out without making radio contact with the sheriff's dispatcher. A sure sign, they later said, that the officer had not stopped the pickup for a violation. That he was only being a good neighbor.

As the lanky 48-year-old deputy approached the driver's-side window of the pickup, the fellow who had been slumped down behind the steering wheel slowly reached over to the glove box and slipped out a .357 magnum revolver. When the sheriff's wide smile appeared in the window, the pickup driver squeezed off the first shot. At point-blank range, he missed.

Instinctively Glenn Smith dived for the ground and crawled desperately toward the back of the pickup, clawing at his own holstered weapon. When the driver opened the door and put his left foot on the ground, the sheriff fired under the pickup, hitting the fellow's boot heel. Rubber flew everywhere, but no blood. The deputy's one shot shook up his attacker, but it did not injure him or slow him down. From the angle of the fatal bullet, investigators later surmised that the driver then surprised the lawman by advancing instead of retreating. From his tenuous position crouched at the tail of the pickup, Glenn Smith looked up just in time to see the gunman step around the end of the truck's bed. The bullet from the .357 magnum took off much of the sheriff's head.

The Killer's Family

"Rupert just killed a man." The wife of a dear friend called me at the church to break the bad news about her brother.

"Rupert did what?" I blurted out.

I had known Rupert Tomlinson for a number of years. Several times I had seen him at his sister's home. A time or two, I think, he'd even come to church with her. But Rupert was not the church-going, family-visiting type. And none of us who had met him were surprised at what he had done. All of us knew he was nuts.

He lived in a tiny, run-down camp trailer parked on an unused strip of public right-of-way in the sleaziest fringe of town. He lived alone, like a hermit, except for one brief period, when a scroungy-looking old mutt shared the squalor of the trailer. With its paint peeling and its tires rotted off and its metal sides dented and dinged, that pitiful old trailer looked almost as bad as its owner. He was a mess. The last time I had seen Rupert, he hadn't combed his hair in a year. Or taken a bath. Or washed his clothes. With his matted uncut red locks filthy and flying, and with his scraggly, scruffy reddish beard masking his raucous mouth, Rupert looked like a wild man. An escapee. A Jack Nicholson look alike. His eyes made my skin crawl. Rupert was crazy.

So I wasn't surprised when his sister phoned me at the church that day.

"Somebody called and told me they heard it on the radio just now," she said. "I'm sure it's him. The news report said he's been arrested and taken to the county jail."

The lady who called me with this awful message was normally quiet and reserved. By the time she finished telling me what had happened, I could hardly hear what she was saying. Her voice was shaky. I could tell she had been crying. Right now she was trying hard to hold back her tears.

"I'll be right there," I told her. And I headed out the church door to be with her family as the full impact of the day's tragedy hit home.

How do you cope with the news that your less-than-sane brother has just wasted a cop? What do you tell your ten-year-old? And your church friends? And the neighbors who until now have always thought you were decent folks?

It's not every day that a family faces this kind of crisis, so there's no routine to follow. What do you need to be doing about it right now? When a family member gets killed, you start dialing long distance to let the rest of the family know what has happened. What do you do when your kinsman is the killer? As I sat with this good family and shared their shock at the incredible events they were being caught up in, I groped with them to identify proper responses to the situation.

Typical of this family's decent and loving spirit was the suggestion of the sister who earlier had called me. "Preacher," she asked tentatively, "how can we tell that poor man's family that we're sorry for what has happened?" I gulped as I saw the answer flash into her mind. "Would you go tell them for us?" What an assignment! To go to the grieving family of a crazed killer's victim. To invade their home in their hour of grief and to try to penetrate their anger and hurt with a message from the killer's family. To tell the weeping widow and the dazed children that the relatives of the killer are weeping, too. That they also are Christians who deeply regret the anguish their insane brother has caused. I've made some tough calls in my day, but that visit that day had to be the toughest of all.

Ranking close to it was my visit to the killer that same afternoon. Rupert's family was concerned about him. They were horrified by what he had done. Shamed and shattered that a member of their own clan could have done such a deed. But he was still their brother, and they worried about how the fellow-deputies of the man he had killed might be treating him. "Will you go see him?" they pled. So I went. Into a jail where anybody who even mentioned Rupert Tomlinson's name drew hostile stares and sullen silence. When they finally brought him out to see me, he was almost as sullen and silent as his captors.

But he was not silent when they hauled him into court. At the request of his frightened sisters, I accompanied them to the hearing. We sat in the front row. Almost close enough to touch Rupert, who came to the hearing with hair tousled. Clothes rumpled. Looking every inch as insane as I had ever seen him. All through the first hour of the hearing he sat glum and unresponsive while the prosecutor's witnesses described the killing as they had reconstructed it from the evidence at the death scene. Rupert refused to acknowledge any comment or question addressed to him. He spoke not one word. Until the recess. The judge had hardly vanished from the bench when Rupert began raving to his court-appointed attorney. "They've got it all wrong," he fumed. "It didn't happen that way at all." And with the entire gallery and the press and the prosecuting attorneys hearing every word, and with his own red-faced attorney trying futilely to shut him up, Rupert poured out a loud and lengthy confession of his crime. At least, as he perceived it. Any Fifth Amendment rights Rupert ever had went down the tubes. All the attorneys, the prosecutor and the defense lawyer and the judge as well, agreed quickly that Rupert was a lunatic. From that point on the hearings and the trial proceedings were only a formality. Within a few days Rupert's address changed from the Maricopa County Jail to the Arizona State Hospital where he was locked up in the ward for the criminally insane.

Rupert's Bible Lesson

Again at his family's request, I visited Rupert there. Every few weeks I would stop by to check on him. Since I was already a regular visitor at the mental hospital, the hospital brass gave me ready access to Rupert. He stayed locked up, of course, but inside the secured ward with a guard just outside the door, we were allowed to visit face to face in a private room. Rupert always seemed pleased when I showed up. He didn't have much company. And he would talk with me quite openly until, almost always, the subject somehow got around to what he had done to the deputy, and why. Then he would begin to scowl, and pointing to the air conditioner grate above our head, he would use hand signals to indicate that he thought the place was bugged. And he would say nothing more.

One day, though, Rupert surprised me. When our conversation drifted into why he had shot the sheriff, he took out a piece of paper and began to write down

Bible verses. Heading the list was Romans 13:4, "He bears not the sword in vain." This verse, linked illogically with half a dozen others, were Rupert's twisted explanation of his violent deed. He had killed because he thought God was telling him to. He saw himself as God's hit man.

When Rupert saw that I understood his explanation, he sat back and smiled the broadest, craziest smile I have ever seen. In his insane way he was absolutely proud of himself for what he had done. Since I was a man of God, he thought I must surely share his estimate of his accomplishment. He had murdered a man for God. And he thought he had Bible verses to justify his actions.

Twisted Scriptures

Wouldn't this world be a better place if maniacs like Rupert Tomlinson were the only people who ever used the Scriptures as a pretext for unspeakable evil? But, sadly, that is not the case.

And it's not just wild men like David Koresh and Jim Jones and Malcolm X who quote Bible verses to validate violence and mayhem. All of my life I've known people who fancied that they were commissioned by God to abuse and misuse other people in His name. Some of the meanest men I have ever known quoted the most Scripture.

Some other time I will tell you the hair-raising tale of the first time I ever encountered child abuse by a Christian parent. That father was an angry, rigid, Bible-spouting man, who cited chapter and verse to explain his gross mistreatment of his beautiful daughter. They didn't lock him up like they did Rupert Tomlinson, but his use of the Bible made Rupert's theology sound almost sane.

Four hundred fifty years ago William Shakespeare observed this warped use of God's words.

> *In religion,*
> *What damned error but some sober brow*
> *Will bless it, and approve it with a text,*
> *Hiding the grossness with fair ornament?*
> — The Merchant of Venice (III,ii,77-80)

Things haven't changed much, have they? Not only can we find some weird soul who will endorse almost any kooky concept with an argument from Holy Writ, but, far worse, we find on every hand men and women who wear the name of Jesus and who still use the Bible to justify hating and berating others who wear the Lord's name. Rupert Tomlinson thought the Bible beckoned him to blow away a man with a cannon. Some of my colleagues evidently feel called to blow away the rest of us with a sermon.

"By this shall all men know that you are my disciples," Jesus says, "if you love one another." What will they know if we don't? What are we saying to the unbelieving world if our standard for good preaching is how little skin we leave on our neighbors who dare to differ with us on minor points of doctrine?

Our Common Gospel

My newspaper reporter friend, Max Albright, called me two or three days before Easter. "I just talked to four clergymen about Easter. I called an Assembly of God pastor," Max said, "and a Roman Catholic monsignor, and the area minister for the Southern Baptists, and a Spanish Disciples of Christ preacher. And all of them said Easter means basically the same thing: that Jesus died for our sins and rose that we might live." In other words, all of them believed the gospel as the apostle Paul defined it in 1 Corinthians 15. If we share this common faith, how can we possibly justify calling each other nasty names and clubbing one another with carefully chosen proof texts? The Bible clearly warns us in Romans 14:10 not to "despise" or to "look down on" a brother for whom Christ died. We have inched uncomfortably close to Rupert Tomlinson's set of mind when we cite other passages of Scripture to justify breaking this one. To explain why God expects us to bludgeon and batter his children with whom we happen to disagree. To affirm our credentials as God's hit men.

Jesus was talking about how his followers should get along with each other when he commanded, "Love one another as I have loved you." Paul was talking about how Christians with differences ought to handle those differences when he commanded, "Receive one another as Christ has received you." Then he added that if we would do that — if we would treat each other right in spite of our differences — it would be "to the glory of God the Father." Jesus says that our oneness in him, our unity despite our diversity, will be the one thing that will convince the world that God sent him. As long as Christians feud and fight and fuss among themselves, the world will miss this saving truth, and our evangelism is doomed to fail.

The Rest of the Story

Today Rupert Tomlinson is a free man. He roams the streets of Phoenix without supervision or restraint. I'm convinced that the psychiatrists who released him more than two decades after his crime must be as nuts as he is. They came to town a long time after the horror of his deed was forgotten by all but a few of us, who will never forget the look in Rupert's eyes that awful day, or the look on that widow's face. For twenty-plus years Rupert was a quiet, soft-spoken, compliant prisoner. He never had been a bully. Or a braggart. Or a trouble-maker. Either in jail, or out. And I'm probably the only human being Rupert ever told about his Bible-based rationale for shooting that deputy. As paranoid as Rupert is, I doubt that he ever let any secular psychia-trist inside that special delusion. So they turned him loose, to putter around the community harmlessly. No threat to anybody. At least, not until he hears from God again. On that day, we can be glad we don't live in Arizona.

Just as Rupert Tomlinson is free, it has been my experience that most of God's self-appointed religious hit men go free. Free from human restriction and free from personal regret. Like Rupert, they blast their neighbors and never once suspect that they have done anything wrong. Some of my sterner colleagues actually seem to be proud of the damage they have inflicted on people they call their "erring brethren." Like Rupert, they see themselves as chosen instruments of heaven sent forth to defend the Kingdom and to chastise God's foes. So they feel holy as they maul fellow-Christians in the name of Jesus. Whether you are a radical Muslim planting a car bomb in Calcutta or a Christian preacher publishing an inflammatory editorial in Kalamazoo, you can go about your dirty work with a clear conscience and with unlimited zeal if you believe you are God's appointed agent performing His will. And all the Scriptures about loving the brethren, and all the meditations like this one, can do nothing to deter the meanness of people who think they are acting righteously on behalf of their God.

So we find ourselves dealing with a paradox that defies solution. Here are honest people with pure motives and with complete dedication to God, who are unleashing hateful, devilish, destructive attacks on the people of God. And doing it with a clear conscience. Just like Rupert Tomlinson. These folks don't mean to be bad. Rupert didn't either. They think they are serving God, just as he thought he was, and, like him, they seem to be totally unaware that they are breaking God's most obvious commandments. These words are not for them. They could never hear what I'm saying.

But it needs to be said. For several reasons. First of all, just as Lt. Smith's family needed to hear that his killer's relatives were sorry for what had happened, so the people who have been savaged by religious leaders with a hit-man mentality need to hear the rest of us saying that we regret this kind of ecclesiastical brutality. They need to know that most of us who wear the name of Jesus disown such hateful behavior and that instead we are trying hard to imitate our Lord's love and mercy. Just knowing this may open the way for God to heal those who have been battered and bruised by pulpit bullies and other church tyrants.

Second, what I am saying here needs to be said loudly enough and clearly enough for our unchurched, unbelieving neighbors to know that most Christians do not condone pulpit abuse. That, in fact, we agree with them that such behavior has no place in any sane religion. If somehow we can convey this message to our unchurched friends, perhaps we will have removed at least one barrier that keeps them from hearing the Good News that Jesus loves them.

And there's a third reason. I would hope that Rupert's story and our reflections on it might cause each of us to be extra careful about how we treat each other. God has not called me to be your judge, or your executioner. He has called me in Christ to be your brother. Surely this must shape what I say to you, and about you. Surely this must soften my criticisms and stimulate my compassion. And if it does — if Rupert's awful deed causes me to be less hateful and more loving — then Glenn Smith did not die for nothing. Then the God who used a Cross to save a world will have used even Rupert's mindless mayhem to impart goodness and grace.

Held Hostage by Fear

"Fear not, for I am with you" (Psalm 41:10).

Can you remember the last time you were afraid? I don't mean just a little bit scared. I mean genuinely terrified. Totally frightened.

I think the person who scared me worse than anybody I have ever known was a 22-year-old woman named Kerri McDaniel. Let me tell you what happened.

"Hi, Kerri," I said when she opened the door. "I'm Gene Shelburne. The preacher from the church you attended Sunday morning. I stopped by to thank you for coming to worship with us."

Back in those days when you could still find somebody at home most of the time, I spent Tuesdays knocking on the doors of people who had visited our church for the first time on the Sunday before. Kerri McDaniel was the fourth name on my list that morning.

"Yeah, I know who you are," Kerri responded without warmth or smile. Her stony face should have tipped me off that trouble was brewing, but I missed the signals.

After all, I had come this young woman's front door to assure her of our church's interest in her. I had come there to try to establish a friendly tie that would bring her back to worship in our pews. My intentions were totally amiable, so I naively assumed that hers were, too.

"Can I come in and visit with you for a little while?" I asked.

"If you insist" are not the words Kerri spoke, but they're a pretty good translation of her guttural grunt and her shrug. She moved back from the door and let me step inside.

I knew at once, before we exchanged another word, that I had just entered the house of a very troubled woman. Just how crazy she really was I was yet to find out, but the room itself told much of the tale.

It was a large room with big airy windows at each end of it, and also across the front of the house. The long wall opposite the front windows had only one door in it, about a third of the way from the left side of the room. Stacked against the remaining two-thirds of that wall, from that door all the way to the right hand corner, were newspapers. In piles. From floor to ceiling.

In this huge room stood only three items of furniture. Out in the middle of the left end of the room was a typewriter on a metal typewriter table with a straight-backed wooden chair. In the open area at the other end of the room was a small sleeper-type divan, the old-fashioned kind where the back of the sofa will lie down flat to form half the mattress alongside the cushion you normally sit on.

When I entered the room, the divan was opened into the sleeping configuration, forming a bed with the mattress top no more than fifteen or sixteen inches above the floor. Where was I supposed to sit down? On her bed?

Kerri maneuvered around behind the open sofa so that it lay between the two of us. She settled her considerable bulk into a sitting position on one corner of the low divan and gestured that I was welcome to perch on the opposite corner. For a skinny fellow with legs as long as mine, this was a far-from-comfortable position. I realized, though, that if I ever hoped to establish any kind of positive tie with this strange young woman, I would have to accept her meager hospitality.

So I sat down. Almost on the floor, it felt like. And struggled all through our visit to keep from sliding off the sloping corner of the rickety old sofa.

Kerri didn't leave me long to worry about the uncertainty of my perch, though. "Why have you been checking up on me?" she snarled. "Why did you call Cled Wimbish to ask about me?" Kerri was angry.

And she was right. I had called my preacher friend across town the day before. At church Sunday Kerri had signed a visitor's registration card. On it she had listed the Broadway congregation way across town as her church home. Since their preacher was one of my closest buddies, I had called him to find out if I needed to pursue the matter any further. I refused to build our congregation by sheep stealing. If this girl was a happy, fruitful member of my friend's church, I would leave her alone and spend my evangelistic energy elsewhere.

So I called him.

"Cled," I inquired, "do you know a woman named Kerri McDaniel?"

In his slow, careful way, Cled replied, "Yes. I know Kerri."

"Kerri showed up in our pews Sunday," I explained. "And I sense that she's a gal with lots of problems. I thought I should touch base with you before I tried to contact her."

"You're on target," Cled verified. And being careful not to reveal any confidential matters he and Kerri had discussed, he briefly reviewed her past few years.

Kerri was a brilliant university student, he told me. Her I.Q. went off the top of the chart. But she was struggling to complete her degree because her school work had been interrupted often by bouts of serious emotional disturbance. Just how serious Kerri's problems really were, Cled did not fully disclose, but he told me he was counseling with her. He urged me to go see her. He said, "She needs all the help she can get."

"Was that Kerri McDaniel?" my wife had asked me after church that Sunday.

"Yes," I confirmed. "Do you know her?"

"I wasn't sure it was her because I haven't seen her for years," Nita said. "Down at the old 5th & McKinley church years ago Kerri and I were baptized on the same night. I wonder where she's been all these years."

Cled's information filled in some of those missing years, but I was not prepared for what came loose that day in Kerri McDaniel's front room.

Why had I been checking up on her? I tried to tell her. Sensing more than normal anger in her question, I tried to reassure her that my call to Cled Wimbish had involved nothing more than the professional courtesy one minister owes another when he's having significant contact with a member of the other man's flock. But Kerri's paranoia had switched into PANIC mode and she was not hearing my assurances. She was a woman controlled totally by fear.

Without missing a beat in her heated accusations, Kerri reached down behind her corner of the sofa and unholstered an enormous .45 caliber revolver. Which never left her hand for the next two hours.

When she gestured, the pistol barrel became her finger. When she lapsed into moodier moments, she caressed the weapon as if it were her only friend. When she was angry (and that was far too much of the time), she waved the gun wildly.

"I keep this thing loaded," she warned me. I believed her. Three nickel-sized holes in the white ceiling above our heads were all that was left of buggers she had blasted during her midnight hallucinations.

For well over two hours, long past the time when my wife and kids expected me home for lunch, I sat motionless on the corner of that dreadful divan, not daring to rise or even to hint that I might be considering something so rash as heading for the door. The thread of Kerri's sanity was so thin, so frayed, that I was afraid my slightest movement might unleash her psychotic fear. Any move could have been my last.

Most of what we talked about during those tense hours I do not remember. Part of the time Kerri told me about her father. And about her school work. And about the fiendish apparitions she saw coming out of her ceiling at night. Every word she spoke betrayed her internal agitation. And her exaggerated fears.

I knew better than to introduce any subject myself, lest I wander unwittingly into the minefields of her paranoid delusions and set off explosions that could destroy us both. So, for two of the most frightening hours of my life, Kerri McDaniel and I talked about whatever subject her demented mind led us to.

My only hope, I realized, was to calm her runaway fears. Maybe if we kept talking I could win her trust — if I was fortunate enough to avoid making some innocent remark that set her off again. Maybe her own verbalizing would ventilate some of her anxiety and reduce her level of internal combustion. Something had to calm her down or I was in big trouble.

My growling stomach told me that noontime had come and gone, but hunger right then was the least of my problems. That gun Kerri kept waving and fondling held my total attention. Finally the rage within her seemed to subside. I could sense that she had tired of threatening me. Something inside her began to relax. When she slid the .45 back into its holster and slowly withdrew her empty hand, I interpreted this as her permission for me to depart. Quietly I dismissed myself and slipped out the door, leaving her still roosting on her corner of the divan.

That was the last time I ever saw Kerri McDaniel. Needless to say, I did not attempt any more house-to-house evangelism at her front door. One dose of that was enough. My preacher friend across town mentioned Kerri to me occasionally when significant changes in her situation brought her to mind. But my own encounter with Kerri was ended. Still, I never forgot her. My heart ached when I read a newspaper account three or four years later of Kerri's violent death.

The four-inch story on Page 27 said she was killed up in the Arizona mountains when a monster truck crushed her ancient VW beetle. Her tormented life was over. I wondered. Was it really an accident? Or was it Kerri's way out?

As I told you at the beginning, nobody ever frightened me more than Kerri McDaniel. But the sad truth is that the real victim of fear on that divan that day was not me. It was Kerri. Out-of-control fear had ruined her life.

When Fear Takes Control

"Don't be afraid," Jesus kept telling people all through his ministry. "Have no fear." This is still one of the most important messages he has for us. Because fear is so disruptive in our lives.

The more frightened I am, the less clearly I think. The more I let fear control my responses to life, the less likely I am to form close and loving relationships. Fear distorts my judgments and poisons my reactions. It is impossible for me to be happy when I am afraid. I need to hear Jesus calling me out of the muddled misery of a life dominated by fear.

Kerri McDaniel's short life was ravaged by fear. Fear that broke its chains and, feeding upon itself, grew into a fiendish monster that terrorized her night and day. For most of us fear is still a pup. A small animal that yaps at our heels and strains at its leash. It annoys us. Distracts us. And tries, as puppies always do, to possess us. But fear, in this small, controllable form, is little more than a nuisance. It can even be a positive thing. A watchdog that warns us of real dangers coming too near.

But some of us can recall times when the puppy grew up to be a mangy mutt. No longer cute and cuddly. Now massive and menacing. The nagging, momentary uneasiness we sometimes felt when we had to be alone in the house at night suddenly turned into an awful terror that threatened to unhinge us. Or maybe the normal anxiety about minor health problems mushroomed overnight into soul-shattering panic when the doctor started hinting that he suspected leukemia. Or malignancy. Or AIDS. Or worse. Then the fear we once controlled with little effort burst all its usual bonds and began to control us. And we were miserable.

Blurred Vision and Blind Eyes

I've had a very recent run-in with fear. On the day after I wrote the last few lines, the vision in my right eye unexplainably began to blur. The letters on the computer screen no longer were clear. I tried moving my head and looking at the screen from several angles. The blurred spot stayed squarely in front of my right eye. When I closed it and used only the left one, everything cleared up, sharp and crisp. When I opened it, everything went crinkly and hazy again.

Except for the normal middle-aged progression into trifocals, my eyes have never really given me any reason to worry. Can you imagine what went through my mind when the vision in my right eye (my only really good eye) suddenly became so fuzzed and distorted that I could not read with it?

That Sunday morning I stumbled and struggled through my scripted sermon. It was an unnerving performance. Hour by hour that day a silent terror began to take over my thoughts. What in the world would I do if this blurring increases and I become unable to read at all? Could I still preach? How would I write? How in the world could I possibly discharge most of the duties that are presently mine each day? If I couldn't drive. If I could not ramble freely from school to church to post office to bank to hospitals to wherever ministry calls? Faced with the possible loss of sight, suddenly I realized just how much my present approach to ministry depends on reading and on mobility. What if I lost those? The very thought chilled my soul.

Several hours spent Monday in the offices of first one doctor and then another offered me some comfort. Along with some consternation. A tiny vein in the back of the eye had stopped up, the ophthalmologist told me, causing blood to leak into the retina of my right eye, impairing the "screen" that normally reflects light rays. Hence the distortion. Just knowing that let me relax some, because it let me turn loose of unbased fears of a dozen worse afflictions.

Knowing the facts is always one of the best antidotes to our exaggerated fears. Most of us have fertile imagination. Usually we can imagine far worse potential woes than the ones we actually are experiencing. So knowledge helps. Facts can banish fears which have no basis. When we're dealing with fear, the words of Jesus certainly work. "The truth *will* set you free."

But the doctor's diagnosis fueled other fears. "Half the time," he told me, "the body will reabsorb the leakage inside the eye, and clear vision will be restored."

My mind instantly churned out the question, "And what about the other half?"

"In those cases," the doctor said, "the distortion

caused by the blood in the retina becomes a permanent condition." He said it might be several weeks before we know.

When I left his office, my medically dilated eyes were still too light sensitive for me to drive safely, so I had to be chauffeured by my wife. And the fear surfaced again: "What if I had to depend on her to take me everywhere I need to go? What would that do to her lifestyle, and to mine?" The possibility is too bleak even to imagine.

I realize now that, like most of our extreme fears, this one at this moment probably is irrational. My left eye does not seem to be threatened. I am not presently facing blindness. Not really. But serious fear seldom pays much attention to reality. Once out of its cage, it tends to gallop unchecked into unexpected areas of our thoughts and emotions.

My purpose in telling you this tale about my eye is not to elicit your sympathy, but to illustrate how fear works on us. Looking back over the years, I realize that this bout with fear was tame compared to the day when my cardiologist stopped my treadmill test and immediately scheduled me for heart catheterization and for possible heart surgery, which he said I was a poor risk to survive. The fact that I actually had no heart trouble — that he turned out to be totally wrong — did not help me in the wee hours that night as I lay in CCU pondering my "last" hours on earth. And I realize that even those terrors may appear minuscule compared to some of yours.

What uncontrolled fear does to us is never a blessing. That's why we need the help of our Lord and the help of our faith to deal with fear.

Of course, a certain amount of fear is healthy and normal for any of us. Normal fears alert us to danger and protect us from harm. But the very fear God intended to bless us is transformed into a destructive curse when it runs amok and takes over our souls. That kind of fear paralyzes and cripples and limits life.

Do you remember what fear did to Lot? After his near-miss with the falling brimstone at Sodom, poor Lot went off and lived like a hermit in a cave because he was afraid to live in a town. Fear put him in a hole. Just like it does us when yesterday's disasters fill today with fright.

Fear damaged Jacob, too. With twenty-plus years to mull over his mistreatment of his brother, Jacob journeyed toward home, and the Bible says he was "greatly afraid and distressed." Although his long-lost brother received him with forgiveness and kindness, fear kept Jacob from ever again being comfortable anywhere near Esau and Esau's army. Just as fear keeps us from trusting and loving and enjoying people to whom we have done wrong.

Famed mountain climber Sir Edmund Hillary, the first man to stand atop Mt. Everest, spoke worlds of truth when he said, "It is not the mountains we conquer, but ourselves."

Living by Faith, Not by Fear

How can we escape our own weakness and rise above the disabling effects of fear? From beginning to end the Bible tells us that the antidote to fear is faith. Faith in a God who is greater than anything or anybody who might harm us. Faith in a God who keeps count of the hairs on our head. Faith in a God whose presence makes us able to confront any foe.

"Fear not," God says to us through Isaiah. "Fear not, *for I am with you.* Be not dismayed, for I am your God" (41:10).

To those of us who are afraid comes the promise, "I, the Lord your God, hold your right hand; it is I who say to you, 'Fear not, I will help you'" (Isaiah 41:13).

Through the prophet Haggai God reminds us, "My Spirit abides among you; fear not" (2:5). *The antidote to fear is the presence of God.*

When our Lord's disciples cried out to him in fear, he responded, "O men of little faith." What was their real problem? They had forgotten who was in the boat with them! They were afraid because they had over-looked the presence of the Lord. Just as we do some-times. When fear replaces faith as the guiding principle of our thoughts and actions, we can be sure that we have begun to depend on our own puny resources and not on the strength of the Lord.

The writer of Hebrews tells us that we who wear the name of Jesus are called by God to "live by faith" and not to "shrink back" when troubles comes our way. If one of us does "shrink back," God says, "I will not be pleased with him." But the writer of Hebrews is quick to affirm, "We are not of those who shrink back and are destroyed, but of those who have faith and keep their souls" (10:38-39). Is this a true description of you? And me?

The ancient psalmist had learned this lesson of faith. "With the Lord on my side I do not fear," he wrote. "What can man do to me?" (118:6). In this same vein the apostle asks, "If God is for us, who can be against us?" Then he acknowledges immediately that all sorts of troubles may descend upon us. War. Sickness. Hunger. Even death. And through all these disasters, he insists, people who know that they have the Lord's love and his presence can be "more than conquerors"! Fear that once melted our hearts and stole our confidence now has no power over us. Not so long as we remain convinced that no danger and no disaster in this world can separate us from the love of God in Christ Jesus. That kind of faith banishes fear.

No Funeral for Ruby

"Honor your father and your mother. . .that it may be well with you"
(Ephesians 6:2-3).

Ruby Milan is the only human being I ever knew who was buried without a funeral. No prayers. No Scriptures. No eulogy. Because her children wanted it that way.

"Get rid of her the cheapest way you can," one of her sons ordered the undertaker who had called to inform him of his mother's death. Just before the son hung up, he added, "Don't call no preacher either. We don't want no fancy funeral. Just bury her and be done with it."

I've often wondered why. What had that poor woman done to deserve so little respect from a son she bore? How had she offended her children? What did she do to alienate them so totally that none of them would drive a hundred miles to attend a funeral or to shed a tear beside her grave?

I suppose I'll never know. But I will always wonder.

In more than three decades of ministry few things have shocked me more than that undertaker's embarrassed apology. "I'm sorry, Preacher," he stammered. "I've never run into a situation like this before."

By rummaging around in Ruby's paltry belongings and by enlisting the aid of the two or three neighbors who knew her, I had helped him find the names of her children so he could notify them of her death. Since I was the only minister involved in this situation in any way, we just assumed from the start that I would handle whatever funeral there might be.

"I don't feel right about this," the undertaker said, "but that son was very specific. 'No funeral,' he insisted. I can't even let you come pray at the burial."

His message stunned me. I couldn't imagine such a thing. How could any family hate their mother that much? Had she abandoned them? Had she abused them? Had she given them grief year after adult year? Only God knows.

I never did meet Ruby's kids, but I still hurt for them and for her. No form of human brokenness exacts a harsher toll on its victims than the rupture of family ties. The wounds a parent inflicts on a child are slow to heal.

A Tough Little Lady

When I first met Ruby Milan, I knew instantly that she was a crusty old gal as tough inside as out. Seventy years of Arizona sun had parched her skin to a leathery, rawhide brown. Seven decades of rough-and-tumble living had toughened and hard-baked her soul as well.

Ruby lived alone in a ramshackle little house in a blighted part of town. An unpaved, dusty road separated her corner lot from that of one of our church ladies. One day when I was visiting Ruby's Christian neighbor, Ruby came to borrow her telephone.

We met that day. Nothing elaborate. Just simple introduction: "This is my preacher. This is my neighbor." She nodded. I said hello. The irreligious bent of Ruby's kids may have been something she taught them. She didn't seem particularly impressed with preachers. At least, not with 25-year-old ones. She was barely polite. She used the phone, and she left.

But Ruby had paid more attention that day than she let me know. "When we're visiting," her neighbor told me some weeks later, "Ruby has mentioned you and asked about you several times. 'Is that young preacher ever comin' back to see you?' she asked the other day. I don't know what's going on in Ruby's mind for sure, but I suspect she's feeling the need to get to know a preacher better, her being past seventy and not well."

Ruby wasn't well. Her wiry, well-tanned Indianesque body did not betray just how sick she really was.

One day her neighbor called to say, "If you're down at County Hospital, Preacher, stop by and look in on Ruby. She went to get some medicine yesterday and her doctor put her in the hospital for tests." I went to see her, because I welcomed the chance to get to know this strange little lady better.

Our visits were nothing spectacular. I showed appropriate interest in her medical situation. She knew little about her problems, or at least she wasn't telling anybody what she did know. But she smiled and seemed genuinely surprised and pleased that anybody would drive all the way south to the ratty old County Hospital just to see her.

In a few days the tests were complete and Ruby returned home. Her doctor's fears had been confirmed. Ruby had colon cancer, and in that day before most of today's cancer therapies were even dreamed of, it did not appear that much could be done for her. All she could do was go home and wait for it to get worse. It did.

"I've Been Robbed!"

One morning at the church I was shocked to receive a call from a head nurse at the County Hospital. "We need your help," she said. "We have a patient who was brought in by ambulance late yesterday." It was Ruby.

"She seems to be out of her head," the nurse told me. "She keeps screaming, 'I've been robbed!', and she won't communicate with us or do anything we ask her to do. We found your card in her purse and thought you might be able to calm her down and get through to her. Can you come to see her?"

I found out that Ruby was not nearly as nuts as they thought she was. She *had* been robbed. On the way to the hospital. By the ambulance driver. And much of her present frenzy was fueled by her fear that other folks in white uniforms might rip off the rest of the treasures she kept stuffed in her beat-up old purse.

Ruby had been unconscious the night before when her neighbor and the police loaded her into the ambulance. Just before they slammed the ambulance door, the neighbor asked the policeman what to do with

Ruby's purse. She was afraid to leave it in the unguarded house. They lived in a rough part of town, and she knew the purse contained all but a few pennies of the Social Security check Ruby had cashed that morning. "Just send the purse along with her," the policeman had advised. "They'll put it in the safe at the hospital."

What the policeman did not know, however, was how many ambulances and how many hospitals Ruby would see before the night was over. In the Catholic hospital Emergency Room, the intake paperwork listed Ruby's possessions. The inventory included an old purse with almost $200 cash in it, my investigations revealed later.

In Ruby's purse, however, they found something else: her welfare card. That meant Ruby was a County Hospital patient. It meant she had no insurance and no funds to pay for her medical care. So the nurses stabilized her and called the County Hospital to send their rickety old ambulance to take Ruby across town where she and poor folks like her belonged.

When Ruby was loaded into the ancient lime-green ambulance, the Catholic hospital records showed she was clutching her purse with its tiny horde of cash. An hour later when she was checked into the E.R. at County Hospital, she still had her purse, but the admitting records indicated it had no money in it.

Ruby was right. She had been robbed. Of all the money she had in this world. Rent money. Grocery money. Money for lights and water and gas. All the money she had to live on for that month. "I've been robbed!" she kept yelling until I finally acknowledged that I knew she was telling us the truth. Then she settled down, content that somebody knew she had been ripped off and would work to set things right. I assured her that I would.

A Dirty Business

Two days later the same head nurse called me.

"Can you come help us with Ruby again?" she begged.

"What's going on?" I inquired.

"She's giving us fits," the nurse groaned. "We can't keep her in bed. We can't keep her clothes on. An hour ago a visitor came to the nurses' desk with a horrified look on her face. She said she had just met a totally naked old lady wandering through the reception area, swinging her colostomy bag and announcing to the world, 'I'm in the manure business.'"

Of course, that was Ruby.

This time she really had flipped. Maybe she was drunk on the painkillers the doctor mercifully ordered. Maybe the cancer had reached her brain. Whatever the cause, she was flying high. For most of that day she was busy and bawdy and bananas.

That night she died.

That's how my life got tangled up with Ruby Milan. A strange little woman I hardly knew, but cannot forget. A tragic woman, whose children wanted her buried without a single word of love or faith or respect.

＊ ＊ ＊ ＊ ＊

"Honor your father and your mother," the Scriptures command. Admittedly, that is not always easy to do. Some parents have treated their families dishonorably. Some have hurt their sons and daughters in unspeakable ways. But even in these toughest of all cases, one mark sets Christians apart from those who do not know God: *Christians work hard at showing honor to their parents.* Down deep inside we feel the rightness of this divine command, and we do our very best to obey it.

In the church we tend to take this for granted. Having lived most of our lives surrounded by people who are respectful and loving toward their parents, we assume that this is the norm for our world.

But we're wrong. Down in the suburbs of Houston, my sister worked for the state of Texas. She was a protective services officer for the elderly. Every week she dealt with people whose treatment of their aged parents would make Ruby Milan's kids look like angels.

Part of the moral collapse in our nation is the loss of responsible, healthy relationships between the generations. Parents abuse and neglect their children, and then the children grow up to abuse and neglect their parents. I suppose that's only fair, but it's a sad state of affairs.

The First Command With a Promise

The Lord's command for us to honor our parents has a promise tacked onto it: *"that it may be well with you."*

In a land where half the kids on any block will grow up hating at least one parent for abandoning them, it is not likely to be well with us.

In an age when incest and sexual abuse leave so many daughters loathing instead of honoring their fathers, it is not well with us.

In a materialistic world so fast-paced and frenetic that many children seldom see their parents and hardly know them, much less honor them, it cannot be well with us.

But it is well for those of us in the Body of Christ, who have somehow dodged the disintegrating pressures of our family-destroying world, and have continued to love and honor the man and the woman who gave us life. Honor for parents is a distinctive element of our faith.

I know our families in the church are not perfect.

I know that Christian sons and daughters sometimes get cross-wise with their mothers and fathers.

All of us know that the church today embraces a host of people whose marriage vows have failed. People who are trying hard this time to get it right.

But in spite of our mistakes and imperfections the high ideal for all of us in the church — even for those who have failed in these areas — is for us to have healthy, honest, caring, stable relationships with the people in our homes. We value family. And it shows.

That's why I was so shocked when Ruby Milan's children wanted her put into the ground unblessed. Because such hostility and crudeness totally violate all our Christian standards for how we're supposed to treat our parents.

That's why we are so disappointed in any church when someone's marriage fails or when some child's misbehavior shames a family and breaks the parents' hearts. Because in Christ we have a higher, holier concept of what family life should be.

Some perverse quirk of humanity makes us pay obsessive attention to our failures while we tend to be blind to our successes. We do that even in the church. We mourn over the divorces and family disasters which have occurred among us instead of focusing on the strength and joy and stability our faith contributes to most of our homes.

Recent studies show beyond all doubt that church people have happier marriages and better-behaved kids than those who don't go to church. Church people, the studies show, are healthier both physically and emotionally than their non-church neighbors. Our children are more likely to succeed in school and in the marketplace.

In today's world it's not easy to be a parent or a child. Poet Merry Browne jotted down some cute lines which say that

> *Parents are people who have photos*
> *For everyone to see,*
> *In compartments of their billfolds*
> *Where the money used to be.*

But the heaviest cost of good family life is not measured in dollars. The true price must be computed in hugs and prayers and tears. Forming and maintaining solid relationships that last requires an immense investment of time and emotional energy. Honor between parents and children grows as the natural result of knowing that somebody else cares that much about you. In today's world of throwaway marriages and transferable kids, Christians committed to keeping their families healthy and whole have a wonderful witness to those around us.

"You are the light of the world," Jesus said to his followers. "You are the salt of the earth." *In a time when major political candidates in a national election cannot even define "family values," the Christian family may well become the envy and the example of our nation.*

If our unbelieving neighbors see our families doing

well while theirs are going down the tubes, they may begin to want what we've got, and that should give us a chance to tell them about Jesus.

Equally important is the hope we can offer to people who have been devastated by mixed-up, messed-up family fiascoes. For those who have known only hate and abuse and fear, the God of all grace offers love and peace and stability. He can bind up our hurts and make us whole again.

***** *

Three years ago my three brothers and I stood beside our mother's grave. Without having planned it ahead of time, all four of us chose to remain behind at the country cemetery when the other mourners headed back to town.

For seven awful months we had watched our mother dying before our eyes. We had seen her victimized and brutalized by a malignant brain tumor and by the modern medical therapies for such a malady.

Now she was at peace. All the words of tribute and honor had been spoken. At two funeral services in widely separated parts of our large state, friends and family had come to say their goodbyes. And now we stayed behind, my brothers and I, to attend to her final need. We filled her grave.

Shovel by shovel we covered her casket with the clean earth. We "tucked her in," as youngest brother Jim aptly put it. Only a few hundred yards from the spot where she was born, still fewer feet from the graves of the parents who gave her life, in the good red soil of the land she loved so fiercely, we put her to bed.

When I was a very young preacher, the way Ruby

Milan's children responded to their mother's death astounded me. I wondered then how any child could be so vengeful. So unnatural. So uncaring. Today I feel sorry for them, because now I know from personal experience how much they missed.

Rebel Poet

"The sabbath was made for man, not man for the sabbath" (Mark 2:27).

An important part of God's answer to humanity's brokenness is the healing, caring fellowship of his church. Sometimes, unfortunately, the church has failed to fill this role. In some cases, in fact, the church has actually caused our brokenness.

What is a person supposed to do if, like my good friend Esther Elliott, she is born into a fellowship walled in by reams of rigid man-made rules, and she is too smart to accept the traditional fiction that these are God's rules? That she can't please God without keeping these rules?

I have a soft spot in my heart for a person caught in this kind of a jam. Maybe that's why I liked Esther Elliott the first time I met her. Even before I heard the saga of this interesting lady's struggle to serve her God acceptably, she stole my heart.

Sometimes it is impossible to please God and man at the same time. Jesus learned this early in his ministry. And Esther Elliott learned the same harsh lesson. Early in her years she butted her head against this hard truth. If you had asked Esther's parents about their teenage daughter, their eyes probably would have dropped and their faces would have clouded as they tried to express the hurt they felt because of their rebellious child. Half a century later, long after her parents were dead, tears welled up in Esther Elliott's eyes as she told me of her conflict with the father she loved. And with their strictest-of-the-strict segment of the Plymouth Brethren.

"Nice girls don't bob their hair," the church elders told all their daughters. Most of them dutifully complied. Not Esther. "Christians girls don't read novels," they legislated. And all the flock avoided the beguiling tales of Charles Dickens and James Fenimore Cooper and Emily Brontë. All of them, that is, except Esther, whose poetic urges were stirring even in those tender years. In fact, the bulk of the discord between Esther and her religious elders grew out of their tendency to distrust and discount education. Her inquiring mind kept tempting her to open books they disapproved. Her love of literature provoked her own father's stern rebuke. Repeatedly.

"To be admitted as a communing member of our fellowship," the church leaders told teenaged Esther, "you must confess your sinfulness and promise to refrain from those sins henceforth." Such sins as wearing makeup. And going to plays. And reading popular magazines. And making friends with young people who were not part of what the elders called "the true church." Unwilling to surrender either her intelligence or her integrity to these stern men with their restrictive traditions, Esther made a choice that upheavaled her parents' world. She turned her back on the church of her childhood. She said "No" to the church of her father. Although he was too angry and too stern to say so at the time, her decision broke his heart. And wounded hers, too. With a wound that never quite healed.

In spite of this early and deep hurt that stayed buried in her soul, Esther Elliott grew to be a saucy lady with delightful wit. A fun gal to be near. When I returned to Indianapolis to preach year after year, somewhere in the week I always made time to visit with Esther. She was retired when I met her, but for several years Esther had worked as a dormitory director at a local religious college. While there she developed a humor-laced friendship with my friend Leo Miller, who was at that time the school's Business Manager. She began to address him in her memos as the school's B.M. This sort of irreverent, ebullient humor made her so much fun to be with.

Less than a year before Esther died, Leo and I drove out to her apartment. For several months she had been in and out of the hospital with heart problems. Evidently she had a premonition that her remaining days were few. That was the only way I could explain what she did. Almost as soon as we got there she began to give us presents. Not expensive, wrapped-in-pretty-paper presents. She gave us items off her shelves and tables. Pictures of people and scenes from her childhood that would have little meaning to anyone except Esther. What-nots and souvenirs which she obviously had kept and treasured from the days when she was a girl.

At first both Leo and I objected. "These are your memories. Your special possessions," we told her.

"That's why I want you to have them," she rejoined. "Because you are the best friends I have in this world, and I want somebody to have them who will value them."

Among the items she gave me were five small black books from her father's library. Four books of Bible studies published in Great Britain in the 1930's for the Plymouth Brethren. And a little song book compiled in 1856 and revised in 1881 by J.N. Darby for use in Plymouth Brethren congregations, *Hymns and Songs for the Little Flock*. Anyone familiar with a modern hymnal can see with a quick glance why "the little flocks" who used this hymnal were likely to stay that way. In a book containing 480 hymns you cannot find one note of music. Only the words are printed. Because the people who used this song book believed with all their hearts that modern musical notation was an innovation of Satan which would seduce their souls and pollute their worship. Where did anybody ever come up with such an idea? Curiously, though, many of these noteless hymns have a nest of numbers on the right side just above the words. Numbers which set forth elaborate metrical patterns for those who knew how to read them. And these formulas for musical rhythm — every bit as complicated as any musical staff or note you ever saw — somehow escaped the prohibitions of these straight-laced people.

As I describe this distinction, which seems inconsistent and odd to most of us today, we should remember that the people who compiled this song book used it to worship God. They were good people. People of faith. I think we can conclude that most of them were not foolish or ignorant. Yet the distinctions and rules which were so important to them seem arbitrary and silly to us. Even as they did to young Esther. Even as some of our own distinctions and rules for worship must seem meaningless and misguided to our religious neighbors.

Is it safe to say that any religious rule not plainly enjoined by the Lord himself is open to legitimate question? Esther Elliott asked questions about the rules of her childhood church. Some of us have raised questions about the rules of our own. Questions like that will almost always get you into trouble with the powers that be, just as they did for Esther.

Banned from her parents' church, Esther began to pour out her searching, emerging faith in poetry that later would be published. She wrote:

> *Can Conflict be ended through Love for each other?*
> *The World is uneasy at best*
> *with Fear going forward, distrust slipping shoreward*
> *on treacherous waves of unrest.*

The uneasiness she lamented in these lines plagued her own soul most of her adult days. Having rejected the rigid ways of family and faith, having elected to walk her own independent road, for most of her life Esther was on her own. She had rejected the "truth" of her father because she was certain that it was not truth. Her search for light and love and right stretched through six decades and through probably twice that many kinds of churches.

In Esther's heart she had a kind of heavenly common sense that had little patience with any church's man-made trappings. In every place she worshipped, she found some goodness. Some value. Some faith worth embracing. But the tendency of all churches to emphasize the trivial and the external invariably turned her off and sent her away in search of believers who honored the Lord more than they honored themselves and their untouchable traditions. Esther was retired and in her late sixties before she finally made enough peace with God and man to seek the baptism offered by any band of believers. As a gray-haired little lady, she at last said "Yes" not only to the Lord she had loved since infancy but now also to the imperfect people who unite to serve Him. And that affirmation, so late in coming, seemed to heal some of the trauma Esther had borne in her heart ever since that fateful day when she had broken with her parents' faith. Thus in her last years she was able to answer the question posed in the poetic lines above:

> *We are all of one favor, one Grace:*
> *Thus, He in His wisdom links brother to brother,*
> *So...PEACE may come only through Love for each other!*

The Fiercest of Loves

Sadly, many of us who are the most religious have learned to love our rules and rituals more than we love God's children.

Jesus crashed head-on into the religious rulekeepers of his day. He rebuked them for "teaching as doctrines the commandments of men." Because he refused to honor their sacred cows and submit to their rituals and rules, they disowned him and laid plans to destroy him. Their approach to serving God was not unlike the way some churches go about it today: even God would get in trouble if he dared to break our rules.

Jesus infuriated one clutch of Pharisees. They challenged him with a choice. Either he could honor their rule against Sabbath healing or he could help a poor fellow with a withered hand. Jesus took their dare. On their holy day, in defiance of their loveless law, he healed the man. And then, having already angered his enemies by his actions, our Lord enraged them further by clearly exposing their double error. They were wrong both in mind and in heart. Their thinking was twisted, Jesus explained, because anybody reading the Scriptures with half an eye open could see that God had always permitted exceptions to the Sabbath rules when trouble arose. They knew that God expected any sensible shepherd to stir himself and rescue a sheep that wandered into a pit on the day of rest. Surely He would permit as much help for a human in distress. Why were the Pharisees too blind see this?

Even worse than his enemies' mental error, Jesus said, was the error in their hearts. They obviously cared more about their rules and their sheep than about this crippled man. Just as those straight-laced church leaders so many years ago cared more about their authority and their rules than they cared about Esther Elliott. Just as we esteem our own traditions and regulations too highly whenever they matter more to us than the people God sends to us for love and light.

Christ's critics that day were sadly mixed up. To correct their distorted values, he gave them a quick Bible lesson. He told them to go learn what God meant when he said through the prophet Hosea, "I desire mercy and not sacrifice." It is a priceless truth. Have we learned it?

Sacrifice as God used the word here does not mean

hardship. It refers in its narrowest sense to the offerings and sacrifices the Jewish priests burned on their altar to worship God. When God says he desires mercy and not *sacrifice,* the word encompasses all the rituals and rules attached to the religion of that day. It is obvious in Matthew 12 that Jesus understood the Hosea quotation to include the Sabbath rules he had just been accused of breaking. How many of our religious rules would the word apply to?

If a divorced and remarried person comes to us, honestly and urgently seeking a renewed relationship with God, what matters more? That all our complicated, impossible rules about divorce and remarriage be obeyed to the letter (according to our peculiar understanding of the rules)? Or is it more important that this earnest seeker find grace and strength and joy in the Lord? Will we prefer mercy or sacrifice?

If a teenager in our church stretches our comfort zone with his music or his wardrobe or his hairstyle, which matters more? That the youngster be forced to conform to the generational tastes of his elders? Or that he find acceptance and encouragement and guidance from the leaders of God's family? If that young person comes to us, will we desire mercy or sacrifice?

Recently I talked with the leaders of a small congregation which had dwindled to a mere handful. The possibility of merging with another small group offered them the double benefit of continuing their witness in that part of the city and of uniting long-divided segments of the brotherhood. "Should we pursue this solution?" they asked me. To do so would require them to violate some of the rules their grandfathers had fought for and would inevitably subject them to criticism. Which was better? To keep the rules rigidly, or to seek unity with others who love the Savior? In the words of Jesus, should they opt for mercy or sacrifice?

The stalwart souls who ran Esther Elliott's childhood church made the wrong choice. They demanded sacrifice. With good conscience and with good intent, they decided that mercy to Esther would be disdain for God. Like so many church leaders since their day, they ignored Hosea. They ignored Jesus. And they turned God's desires upside down, electing not mercy, but strict obedience to all their sacred rules.

I tell you the sad tale of those stern men not to throw rocks at them. They did the best they knew, and God alone must judge them now. How sad it will be if, as Jesus said, the measure they gave is the measure they get! How sad for all of us, who depend totally on God's mercy, if we show no mercy to those who come into conflict with our system of rules.

I tell you Esther's story because I have discovered that the world is full of Esthers. In every community are a host of souls who carefully avoid all contact with churches and preachers because they have been battered and bruised by the Keepers of the Rules. Like beaten pups, these people flinch today at the slightest mention of church. On some dark day in the past, when they were weak and disobedient and confused, church leaders condemned them. Church people rejected them. In the name of the God of mercy, church officials laid down rules which were humanly impossible for them to comply with. So these people left. Like Esther, they walked away. And many of them, expecting no mercy from Christians, have not yet found their way home.

If you doubt what I'm telling you, visit any

Alcoholics Anonymous meeting in town. Talk to men and women whose lives came apart because of their alcohol abuse. Ask them how their churches treated them when they began to slip toward disaster. When they began to violate the rules of the Christian fellowship they belonged to. Seldom will any of these people tell you about compassion and mercy shown by Christians. Instead they will often tell you about blame and criticism and rejection. That's how churches tend to treat people who break their rules.

Let me hasten to say that most of the rules these alcoholics broke were wise rules they should not have broken. God's rules are always made for our good. As Jesus said, "The Sabbath was made *for* man." God seeks only our happiness when he says, "You shall not commit adultery." He intends to bless us when he outlaws drunkenness and disorderliness and divorce. As my alcoholic friends recover, most of them recognize the rightness of the rules. Just like we do. They know today that the immoralities of their drunken pasts wounded them and their loved ones. They know that their alcohol-related divorces caused untold pain. They are smart enough to see that their past irresponsibilities hurt every life they touched. They would have been infinitely happier had they been able to live by the rules.

But they couldn't. Because of human weakness — because of what Paul called "the law of sin and death at work in their members" — they sinned. Now that they have messed up so badly and want to get their lives straight again, what should be the church's response? Will we hold them forever, eternally, unforgivably responsible for the rules they broke? Will we demand sacrifice? Or will we join our Lord Jesus in extending mercy? Will we welcome them to wholeness? Even if some of the rules have to bend a bit.

"The Son of man is Lord of the Sabbath," Jesus tells us. In other words, he is saying, "I'm in charge of the rules. I am the One who can give you permission to break the rules while you save a sheep. I'm the One who can allow you to set aside the rules while you save a sinner." And he insists, "I desire mercy, not rule-keeping."

In Jesus' eyes, people always matter more than rules. And broken people always matter to him most of all.

Satisfied With My Sins

"Let us throw off. . .the sin that so easily entangles" (Hebrews 12:1).

Why is it that we become so content with our own bad habits and wrong attitudes and sins?

Does it bother you that we who worship the sinless One often see no reason to get rid of our own sin? Instead we find reasons to justify our gluttony, our anger, our laziness, and our pride. Amazing, isn't it? Since these are the flaws that cause our health to fail and our happiness to disintegrate.

"If your eye causes you to sin," Jesus tells us, "pluck it out and throw it away. It is better for you to enter life with one eye than with two eyes to be thrown into the hell of fire" (Matthew 18:9). Jesus gives no quarter to sin. Why do we?

Why do we so often elect to live imperfect, broken lives when he wants us to be whole? Why are we will-

ing to be so much less than He wants us to be, less than
He died for us to be?

To answer these perplexing questions, let me tell
you a parable.

*   *   *   *   *

"Ethel wants you to drop by her place," one of our
church ladies told me.

More as a question than as a comment, I replied to
the woman on the phone, "I wonder what she wants?"

"I don't know for sure," my caller responded, "but
she mentioned that she was not feeling good and I think
she wanted to see you right away."

An hour later I parked by the curb in front of Ethel's
place.

This was my first visit to her home. It may very well
have been the first time anybody had visited Ethel's
home — at least within a decade. Her invitation still
very much surprised and puzzled me, because Ethel
didn't strike me as the sort of person who hankered for
much company.

Everybody in the Sunnyslope community knew
Ethel. I doubt that a dozen people knew her name, but
everybody knew her by sight. She looked for all the
world like a witch. Like a classic hag out of a
Halloween carnival or out of a story like Snow White.

In summer and winter she wore a heavy black shawl
draped over the top of her head and trailing in the dust
at her feet. Cinched up beneath her chin, the shawl hid
her hair like a nun's habit and splayed out to swath her
stooped form. All that was visible of Ethel was her hag-
like features — her beak nose and her protruding chin
and her leathery face stained indelibly gray by the ashes

and soot deposited in the deep wrinkles on her narrow forehead and her high cheek bones.

As a girl Ethel probably stood five-five or six, I would guess. She was so bent and bowed down by the time I met her that I doubt she measured four feet from sole to crown. As she shuffled along the city's thoroughfares with her black shawl dragging in the dust, hiding her short, quick steps, she looked like a ball of dirty black wool floating (perhaps on a concealed broom?) along the road's edge. Everybody in the neighborhood had seen Ethel.

The first time I met Ethel she knocked on the door of the lady whose phone call I started telling you about. We were studying the Bible with one of this lady's neighbors that afternoon, when Ethel rapped on the side door of the house.

"Would you like to buy a pretty potholder?" Ethel cackled.

I didn't learn until later that Ethel bummed the potholders from the benevolent manager of a nearby five-and-dime store and then sold them to folks in that neighborhood for twice their original price. That day, looking at Ethel for the first time as my hostess graciously invited her to return at a better time, I was dumbfounded. I had never seen a real, live creature quite like her.

Ethel did come back. Every Tuesday afternoon for almost a year we studied Bible in that house, and Ethel, who lived only two or three blocks away, reappeared on several of those days. She came often enough and stayed long enough that she got to know me as her nice neighbor's preacher. And for some reason that I never knew, she took a shine to me.

Hence, the phone call which drew me to her door. Ethel didn't know my telephone number. She probably did not even know where my church was. So she had her Christian neighbor, who did know all those things, to summon me to her hovel.

Hovel is probably too mild a word. Ethel lived in the most run-down shack you ever saw. It had only one small room, I found out. And Ethel never used the front door, I also found out that day. It was not hard to see why.

When I rapped on Ethel's front door, I heard a rattling sound like a jillion tiny pebbles plunking on parchment and sliding off. Then everything got quiet. So I knocked again. The frantic rustling noise resumed, this time punctuated with thuds and bumps, sort of like kittens jumping from table tops. Then all was still and silent again.

I was turning to leave, assuming that Ethel must out prowling around the community somewhere, when I saw the front door shimmy ever so slightly. How many years it had been since that door had been opened only God knows; it took Ethel several tries to get it unstuck and to pry it open just far enough to peek out and to instruct me hoarsely to come around back.

I never did really get inside the house, I'm glad to tell you, but I did find out what had caused all the noise when I knocked. Piled from floor to ceiling in the whole shack with only a tiny path snaking from front door to back were old newspapers and paper sacks covered with dust and soot. The slightest unusual movement anywhere near the shack activated an army of huge cockroaches, and any major disturbance set in motion the rats and mice who perched unmolested on shelves and boxes and stacks of rubbish in the house. Ethel lived in that.

On cold days like the one when I came to see her, Ethel squatted on a rusty old stool just inside the partially open back door of the house, and fed scraps of apple boxes to the fire in a small cast iron stove with a stopped up flue. Smoke drifted out the top of the open door and soot from the fire settled gritty-gray on everything in the shack, including Ethel. A half-opened can of pork and beans sat bubbling and caked over atop the tiny stove. It was Ethel's lunch.

"Doris told me you needed to see me," I began the conversation as I looked in amazement at a 1929 Ford with no wheels, flat on the ground, about five feet from the back door. Every square inch inside it was stuffed with junk Ethel had crammed into it.

"Yes," Ethel answered. "I need some help and you're the only person I can trust."

Just how I had gained that kind of confidence from this suspicious old lady, I was not sure, but I inquired, "What can I do for you, Ethel?"

"I'm sick, Preacher. Bad sick. I've got to go to the hospital, but I can't leave my place here with all my belongings. When they know I'm gone, they'll rob me blind."

Just who "they" might be was never clear, and what in the world anybody would want to steal out of her rubbish heap I could not imagine.

"What are you afraid of losing, Ethel?"

"My money," she moaned. "If I go to the hospital, they'll steal all my money."

I remembered that some of the neighbors had speculated from time to time about what Ethel might have stashed in her shack, but in their wildest moments not one of them would have dreamed what that old lady really had there.

"Here, Preacher!" she begged. "Help me count this."

Out of the old purse she always hauled around she dumped a pile of crumpled greenbacks and a fistful of crinkled envelopes containing Social Security and welfare checks. Many of them unopened. I couldn't believe my eyes. Together we counted more than $8,000.

Wary of being entrusted with that much money by an obviously paranoid stranger, I gingerly broached the subject of what *we* could do to safeguard *her* money. "I want you to take care of it for me, Preacher," she cut me off, "but this ain't all of it."

From the roach-rattling newspaper mountain behind her she extracted several ratty old purses and tattered shoeboxes. As she shook out their contents, the pile of money and uncashed welfare checks grew. Before we finished that backdoor audit, Ethel had unearthed more than $18,000.

"Ethel, I'm just like you." I mustered all the persuasiveness I possessed. "I would be afraid to have that much money lying around unprotected, especially if it wasn't mine. I'm not sure I could hide it as well as you have."

She nodded.

Expecting quick rejection, I tiptoed up to the question, "Ethel, have you ever thought of putting your money into a bank?"

Ethel grunted and began rummaging through the stack of old purses. Imagine my relief and astonishment when she produced a faded old passbook embossed with the name of a bank less than a mile away. The last balance in the passbook, without any interest credited for nearly two years, was more than $12,000.

"Ethel, why don't we take all this money" — I pointed to the pile of loot next to her stool — "why don't we take this and deposit it in your account down at the bank? Would that be all right with you?"

"Yeah," she agreed, "but you'll have to take it down there for me. I'm too sick to make it that far."

So into the bank I sauntered that day with a rumpled, faded paper sack in hand, and deposited four times my annual salary at that time — more money, in fact, than my three-bedroom house had cost — into the account of a spinster who lived on rancid food out of tin cans in a hovel I would not house my dog in.

"Ethel can do better than this," I thought to myself as I hurried back to return her passbook and her deposit receipt. "Ethel doesn't have to live in these shambles. She certainly does not need to spend her days begging. Even if welfare finds out that she is wealthy and cuts off her monthly checks," I calculated, "she has enough money in the bank to pay ten years of rent in a clean, decent apartment. With just a little help, life for Ethel can be a whole lot better."

Ethel was right. She was sick. During the days she spent in the county hospital at taxpayer expense, her Christian neighbor and I set about to liberate Ethel from her run-down shack.

"Ethel needs somebody to take care of her for a few weeks," the hospital people told us. "She's too weak and tottery to be at home alone." None of them had seen her home, of course. They imagined a nurse or a housekeeper caring for Ethel in a normal residence. In Ethel's rat-trap such care was out of the question, so we contacted her welfare worker.

"Can you help us find some decent place where Ethel can receive the meals and the care she can't provide for herself?" we asked.

"You bet I can!" she beamed. "I've been trying to get Ethel out of that shack for several years. This is the perfect chance." Within a week the welfare lady had located a dandy place, not a nursing home as such, but a supervised apartment not too far from Ethel's old neighborhood. It was ideal! At least, that's what *we* thought.

I was not with them when they transported Ethel from the hospital to her new home. I wanted to be. I wanted to see the look on her face when she found out that her new house had central heating and air conditioning. I wanted to hear what she said when she found out that for the first time in years she would have running water and a working bathroom inside her living quarters. I could imagine her pleasure at having clean floors and lighted rooms and a refrigerator and a T.V. and a litter-free lawn. She had to feel like a queen in a new palace.

Anything I imagined was wrong. Ethel couldn't stand the place. The county was paying her whole tab — lodging and meals, the whole smear — but as soon as Ethel had strength enough to navigate, she vanished. A week later neighbors saw smoke rising from Ethel's old back door. She was home again, cooking rotten canned food and warming herself by the boxwood fire, restoring her personal coating of soot and ashes which the hospital people had scrubbed off of her. There, among the rats and the roaches and the rubbish, Ethel was at home and happy.

In the months that followed various welfare workers and social agencies called upon us several times to help them relocate Ethel. That she was living in subhuman accommodations was apparent to everybody except Ethel. They rented her several nice apartments, places located nearer to her old haunts where they fancied that she would feel more at home. I don't think she stayed in one of them more than two days before she returned to her smoky hovel.

The lumber yard whose property adjoined Ethel's on the east offered her a handsome price for her place, more to remove the eyesore next door, I guessed, than because they had any real need for the land. With that money added to her cache at the bank, she could have lived out her years like a princess. She turned them down flat.

Neighbors turned out en masse the day Ethel's shack caught on fire. Sparks from her defective stove ignited her piles of paper. Firemen literally covered the lot with partially burned trash they dragged out of the hut after they had doused the blaze. Nearby residents who could not stand Ethel's garbage-dump decor rued the fact that the firemen were so efficient. Others watched disappointedly to see if the poor firefighters dodging rodent and roach attacks would unearth any of Ethel's fabled treasures.

When the fire was out, the electricity company disconnected power to the house and cut away the melted wires. "That's it," we all thought. "Now Ethel surely will have to abandon this mess." "There's just no way she can live here now," her Christian neighbor told me. But Ethel and her junk-heap house were far too attached to be separated by a little fire. A day or two later she was ensconced once more on her backdoor perch, seemingly oblivious to the piles of charred debris strewn haphazardly all over her lot.

And that's where she was the last time I saw Ethel. All of us who knew her were trying to clean her up and improve her life, but Ethel stayed put. For a very simple reason: She liked the mess she lived in.

✱ ✱ ✱ ✱ ✱

So do we.

"In my Father's house are many mansions," Jesus tells us. But most of us are like Ethel. We prefer our shacks.

I know a woman who spends much of her time telling people how badly her father molested her three decades ago. For thirty years she had chosen every day to re-kindle her anger and recite her hatred for a man who, tragically, is not sorry for what he did and who does not intend to change. She doesn't intend to change either. To give up her anger, to say, "I forgive the man who wronged me," would cause her to move from a hovel full of hostility to a place full of love and peace. But hatred has been her home for thirty years and, like Ethel, she likes it.

"Some individuals hug their hurts," Gary Gulbrantson writes. "The only way they have been able to gain significance is by drawing attention to their problems." Is this why some of us are so slow to master our weaknesses? If our spiritual wounds were healed, then we would lose the right to expect others to carry our load.

One time Jesus came to a man who had been lame for forty years. "Do you want to be whole?" Jesus asked him. "Of course, I want to be well!" we expect the man to roar in reply. But maybe he didn't. Maybe he was like Ethel. Maybe he liked his pallet by the pool. Maybe he liked the wretched society beside the waters of Bethesda. Maybe if he let Jesus touch him, he would lose the misery he had come to enjoy.

And what if Jesus were to touch us and make us whole? What would we lose?

What if His saving touch were to remove from our hearts the lust that fuels our fantasies of sexual delight? Would we like to live without them?

What if He touched us and took away the self-pity that shapes our daily view of who we are and of how family members treat us?

What if Jesus came to those of us who for years have been addicted, and asked us, "Do you want to be well?" What would we tell Him? Do we really? Or are we, like Ethel, quite content with the mess we're in?

The Bible talks about those who "persist in sin" (1 Timothy 5:20). It talks about sin "which clings so closely" (Hebrews 12:1). It talks about those who are "enslaved to sin" (Romans 6:6). These are true and accurate descriptions. As Paul said in Romans 3:9, "All men are under the power to sin."

The question is whether we want to stay there.

Before our Lord Jesus was born, the angel said, "He will save his people from their sins." Every Lord's day we Christians gather to worship Him and to celebrate the fact He died to do that. On the cross He gave his life and His blood was shed to set you and me free from sin.

But Jesus, you see, will treat us better than we treated Ethel. He'll leave us right where we want to be.

He wants us to be moral. He wants us to be clean. But Jesus won't force us to be. The choice is ours. The ball is squarely in our court.

The Lord will not evict us from sin. He will not bodily force us out of our bad habits. He will not make us give up our wrong attitudes. He will not pressure us to reform. That's the genius of the gospel. God's saving grace is offered to those who can freely choose to accept the gift or to walk away.

We can be set free from the sins which pollute our lives — unless, like Ethel, we're so much in love with the mess we're in that we reject the efforts of Heaven itself to lift us up to a better, cleaner, nobler life.

Most of us have to make that choice every day.

In Jail With John

*And John, calling to him two of his disciples, sent them to the Lord
saying, "Are you he who is to come, or shall we look for another?"
... And Jesus answered them, "Go and tell John what you have seen and
heard: the blind receive their sight, the lame walk, lepers are cleansed, and
the deaf hear, the dead are raised up, and the poor have the good news
preached to them. And blessed is he who takes no offense at me" (Luke
7:19, 22-23).*

In at least three stages of life our dreams turn to ashes.
    Then the flames which normally fire our souls and
        give meaning to the struggle burn perilously low.
    Then certainties which blaze in the words of a man
        like the Baptizer, in those days of self-doubt, blur
        and cool, and the bold pronouncements are
        replaced by silence.
        Tentative. Self-accusing. Terrible.
        Silence.
Only the most blessed — or the most blind — fail to go

through these valleys of near-death when life has
lost its luster and all its exclamation marks have
wilted and now look like questions.

*"Behold the Lamb of God who takes away the sin of the
world!"*
*"Is this the One who was to come, or shall we look for
another?"*

Three times in the life of a man or woman we are in
danger of this dreaded immolation of our hopes and
dreams.

"You will deny me thrice," was foretold not only
of Peter, but of all who wear the Name.
A young friend of mine — a man of the cloth who
ministers in a fellowship which distrusts and
prohibits the cloth — came to me to pour out his
soul's agony. At 25 he was mired, without knowing
it, in the first trough of human despair.
He was perched on the ash-heap of his youthful ideals
and his boyhood ambitions.
Like John on the banks of Jordan, he had set out to
call a lost world to accept Jesus.
Dressed in the rude raiment of a poorly paid parson,
he had sallied forth to decry the sins of the
shameful and the shams.
Locusts and wild honey would be diet enough for
one so full of zeal, so sure of God's call.
"I'm not sure I believe it anymore," he confessed to me
hesitantly, as if he thought heaven's bolt might
strike, or the earth might open to swallow and
squelch such a confession.
"Not believe *what*?" I wondered to myself. Just how
deeply into his faith has doubt penetrated?

I remembered the turmoil of my own soul at his age. A
pastor with no pastor. A tormented child of faith
with no father of the faith who could be trusted with
the revelation that I was beginning to question the
Unquestionable in our fellowship.

Thank God this young friend felt free to tell me,
although with fear.

"How do we *know* that the Bible is true?" he begged for
assurance. "Can we really be as sure as we seem to
be about miracles and prophecies and Gospel
events?"

Now he had said it.

"Is the Lamb of God really the Lamb of God?"
"Is the baptizing in the Jordan really from heaven?"
"Was I all wrong to begin with?"

His doubts were more serious than mine had been at
his age. No more painful, I think. Not a bit more
debilitating to present ministry. No more damaging
potentially to his professional future. But more
fundamental, for sure.

My early doubts had dealt more with peripheral
matters of ritual and relationships with other believers who weren't as "right" as we were. But I remember like yesterday that my questionings left me feeling the same as my young friend:

hypocritical before a congregation who thought I
shared every prejudice and precept in their
multiplied hearts, and

ill-suited to proclaim a message of faith when I
myself found so much that for that moment
was hard to believe.

This young preacher at least was smart enough to dive

past surface issues and plunge to the core of faith — to ponder the terrifying question of whether he was a believer in the most basic sense of the word.

My heart ached for him.

In his youth he had no way to know that the wheels come off of life for most people in their mid-twenties.

> Young ministers are not the only ones who leave the Jordan and lose sight of the dove.

> Fledgling doctors, apprentice ditch-diggers, third-year math teachers, and GS-4 civil servants have this in common: this painful period of self-questioning, when the brilliant flames of teen-age dreams are damped and guttered by the stark realities just now seen in the harsh adult world.

Twenty-five is a bad time to be alive. I remember.

> Is this the profession I really want to spend my life on, or should I look for another?

> Is this the man (or woman) I want to sleep and eat and commune with all my days, or should I look for another?

> Is this the church I want to support and attend and struggle with from now on, or should I look for another?

> John's question haunts us in early adulthood.

Must all the former certainties of my life be flushed away if I am to deal honestly with today's doubt?

Twenty years later — give or take five — the fires of life burn low again.

> It's not just a matter of estrogen either.

Middle-age crazies are evidence of imbalances
far more basic than body chemistry.

The Jordan of youth is now long past. A dim memory.
Was it ever more than a dream?

Most of us by forty-five have gone to jail with John.

Unbending and impenetrable are the bars of the
prisons we have entered.

Prisons of professions so successful we now
could not possibly change.

Prisons of financial arrangements at once too plenti-
ful and too pitiful for us to bobble in our tight-
rope routines.

Prisons of habits and tastes and ailments
bundled together inseparably by half a life of
living. To change them would be to stop
being us.

From behind the bars we plaintively wail John's question.
Is this what was to come?

Is this marriage, this line of credit, this church,
this leisureless rat-race, this loneliness, this bitter
taste, this day just like so many yesterdays — is
this what was to come?

Somehow in the heat of the corporate struggle,
somehow in the frenetic pace we called family life,
somehow in the thoughtless rush through the
prime of life —

we expected the prize for the race to be worth it all.
We expected something special.

Instead, we got *this*.

Is *this* what was to come?

I did not tell my young preacher friend that he was not
the only clergyman in the room with uncertainties in
his soul.

Was I less than honest?

I did not tell him that some days at forty-six the future of my own ministry (always a lifetime commitment for me) was up for grabs.

How could he, who one day contemplates Law and the next day opts for medical school as possible new, exciting careers — how could he possibly understand if I tell him that only two days before our visit my own despondent, downcast steps trudged through the city streets in search of job possibilities for one now too old to fantasize any longer about Medicine or Law?

Assurance this young man needed from me. Not middle-aged doubts.

Before him lie years of fruitful ministry and solid service — once he has rekindled the Spirit's fires and forged for himself new and truer convictions.

> Then he will tuck away his second-hand sermons and preach to his people what he has seen with his own eyes — that the lame walk and the lepers are cleansed and the dead (and doubting) do come to life.

> Then he will bear faithful, firsthand witness to the difference Jesus makes when we let him touch our souls.

Knowing this, I gave this young man love. Not criticism. Not censure. I loved him, doubts and all, and led him toward new faith down the oft-trod avenues of his own keen mind.

"What reasons do you have to trust the words of Scripture?" I asked him. Because I knew that he knew.

> His answers took shape. Slowly at first. But with

gathering weight and quickened pace. He had studied carefully. His questions had not been superficial. Painstakingly in the Holy pages and through the writings of others who questioned before him, he had sought for the substance and sureness of God.

Make no mistake. His doubt drove him toward God. Not away. Just as the doubts of John in prison sent him *to* Jesus for assurance.

My young friend came back — like John's friends — with the right answers.

Confirmation, the Lutherans call it. This young minister was not 12 years old, but he *was* confirmed.

He did not need to know just now that his newly firmed up faith would shake again in two decades — this time not because of doctrinal dilemmas but because of a new identity crisis triggered partly by looming mortality and partly by sagging midlife self-esteem.

It would not help him in the least for me to inform him that he really won't become a Robert Schuller or a Billy Graham.

In his own time he'll find his own way to rationalize about the worth of an unseen ministry to a handful of people in a small town.

His ministry won't be improved a bit if so soon I reveal to him the bitter realities of all ministry:

— that some to whom he gives the most will appreciate him the least,

— that some for whom he endures the most will be most likely to resent him.

Twenty years from now he will know. That will be soon enough.

Until then let him enjoy the fire of the bush that
burns so brightly when the Lord is present
within.

Let him know warmth of heart and soul before
the ashes come again.

They will come. A third time, I am told.

But I haven't been there yet. I really don't know.

Some twenty years more, when retirement is reality,
and all the glorious plans of ease and play and
leisure and loafing turn out to be one vast desert of
boredom and loneliness —

then again the ashes of life-dreams sift through
our disillusioned fingers.

Can the fire then be lit once more — as it was twice
before in our lives? Can it burn brightly and excitedly
as it did in earlier days?

I think so — if then we have someone to love us and
to lead us as they did before when life went flat, and
joy fled, and all seemed futile for awhile.

✻ ✻ ✻ ✻ ✻

What a pity if we double our depression by blaming
ourselves when we awake in one of life's valleys!

Disappointment and doubt are no more sinful than
pain or paralysis.

Right on the heels of John's question came Jesus' finest
commendation.

Not *condemnation*. Not criticism.

Jesus praised this mortal who dared to speak his doubts.

"Are you the One who is to come?"
*"Of all those born of woman, no man is greater than
John."*

> That's what Jesus said.
> Even with his temporary doubts.
> Even when his life seemed ill-spent.
> Even when he thought of having to start all over again.
> Even then — John received our Lord's high praise.

But Jesus reserved his highest praise for doubters like you and me.

John may be great —

> *"But the least in the kingdom of heaven is greater still."*

✷ ✷ ✷ ✷ ✷

One last reflection.

If we are in jail with John —

> We who just tasted the rigors of adulthood.
> We who burned out at midlife.
> We who lived sixty-five years to get something we don't really want.

If we are in jail with John, *how do we get out?*

> Just like he did.

We die.

We die to our self-pity and our hostility and our pride.

We put to death the old man — the carnal part of us — that keeps coming alive to make us covet and envy and value the wrong things.

We crucify the flesh, with its wrong-headed wants.

> That's the only way to walk away from our self-constructed jails.
> We must die so Jesus can make us alive.

When You're Broken
and Don't Know It

"God gave them up to dishonorable passions. Their women exchanged natural relations for unnatural" (Romans 1:26).

At the very heart of the Christian gospel, filling that Message with hope and joy and relief, is the grand truth that when we are broken, God will put us back together again.

That's what the early Christians called "the Good News." "After you have suffered a little while," Peter promised, "the God of all grace . . . will himself restore, establish, and strengthen you."

For people whose lives have come apart, this is a glorious Message. Our messes can be cleaned up. Our brokenness can be healed. No failure is too great for God's grace. No mistake too serious to be forgiven.

That's what Jesus sends us to preach. To men and women battered by divorce, tormented by addictions, humiliated by failures, ruined by poor judgment — to people whose lives and hearts are broken — we proclaim a Message of wholeness and healing and strength: *Our God will put us back together again.*

But what Message do we have for people so entangled in sin that they don't even know they are broken?

What would Christ have us say to people like my friend Lana?

Lana called me last month. At the moment I wondered why.

It had been at least a year since I had seen Lana. A chance meeting then. At her parents' home. I had been visiting briefly in their home, swapping tales about grandkids and catching up on family developments. The way close friends do when they don't see each other more than once or twice a year.

Their son had just changed jobs. Their youngest daughter had just had twins. They were just home from New England. So were we. The color of the leaves was incredible, wasn't it? And the Maine lobster out of this world. Did they make it to Kennebunkport? You know the kind of conversation I'm describing.

So much to share in so short a time, so we flit from one topic to another like hummingbirds that can't decide which flower's nectar to dabble in next. Like friends, who enjoy everything about each other, and in a short visit can't possibly tell enough or hear enough to be satisfied.

Living much too far away in western Kentucky, Lana's parents are among my dearest friends. Over the years we have traveled together, worshipped together, done business together. As only best friends can do, we have laughed hilariously, and wept unguardedly, and shared dreams and hurts and fears.

Lana ducked into her parents' living room that afternoon, she and her twelve-year-old daughter. They had blown into town to see an old school chum, I think she said, and to take care of some business there in Lana's hometown.

She and the daughter now live alone in the big city 150 miles farther south and east, where she has a good job in a large investment firm. If promotions mean anything, her bosses like her. She has risen fast. I have observed Lana ever since the days long hence when she was her daughter's age. Her boundless energy must be a real asset in her fast-paced career. Demands that would swamp the average gal just prime her adrenalin flow and enhance her performance. I'm sure she's good at what she does.

That day when she poked her nose through her parents' front door, we didn't talk much. Just warm greetings flung at each other on the fly. "Hey! What a grand surprise!" I exclaimed to her. "How in the world are you?"

"Just great! And you?" Lana's voice always surprised me, with its aggressive, mannish timbre.

"Couldn't be better," I replied. "Who's that grown-up kid following you around?" Twelve-year-old Gina grinned. I don't think she quite knew what to make of this old codger who was being so familiar with her mama. She had seen me often when she was much younger, but several years had passed and I doubt she now remembered exactly who I was.

Two or three more quick lines were bandied between us. Then Lana and her child flew out the door in a mad dash to some place they were supposed to be. Just like old times. Lana had always been racing somewhere. Always ten minutes later than she should have been. Because she always scheduled two things more than a body could possibly do in every hour. That was Lana way back when. And she obviously hasn't changed.

That was the last time I had seen Lana before the telephone rang in my study last month. On the other end of the line, sounding like she might be next door, Lana greeted me with her distinctive voice. Instantly I knew who it was and my heart quickened a bit as I wondered why she was calling.

Her father's health is precarious. Has been for years. Has he had another heart attack? I wondered in that instant before she launched into the call. *Is she calling to tell me we need to plan a funeral?*

I don't know if normal folks think like that, but preachers do. Especially when they were the one who received the first call from miles away when the earlier catastrophe struck. We're used to being called in moments of crisis. Could that be why Lana was calling me?

No. "Dad and Mom are fine," she assured me. "They're off on a trip somewhere. Tennessee, I think. They sounded good on the phone last night."

But something was wrong. I could sense it in Lana's voice. And in the tentative way she made small talk. She had something to ask me. Or to tell me. I wasn't sure which.

Maybe she had decided to get married again. The thought flashed through my mind. *Maybe she wants me to perform her wedding.*

Wrong again. Way wrong!

"Have Mom and Dad talked to you about me?" Finally Lana tiptoed up to the subject. She seemed surprised when I told her no.

Not since the rocky days of her divorce half a dozen years before had her parents and I talked much about Lana's problems. Lana herself had called me then. Often. When the turbulence and depression and anger of her disintegrating marriage had almost engulfed her. More than once back then Lana had called me from halfway across the state to pour out her distress and to validate tough decisions she was having to make in the eye of an emotional hurricane. But those stormy days had passed and since that time her folks and I had seldom mentioned Lana's concerns. They bragged about each new job she got and, like any good grand-parents, they kept me informed of their granddaugh-ter's notable achievements, but in recent years this had been the extent of our conversations about Lana.

"Your mom told me about your newest job promo-tion," I told Lana as I scanned my memory, "but I think that's all I've heard about you in the past year or so."

"I really thought they would have told you," Lana plunged into the heart of the conversation. "But that's why I called you. I want you to know that I'm gay."

Then she waited. Listening. Apparently wondering what I would say.

What would you have said?

Not many weeks before Lana called I had read the finest statement I have ever seen outlining a Christian response to homosexuals. So much of what Christians have written or preached on the subject sounds hateful and hard. We have used words like bricks to bash those who are struggling with homosexual inclinations. Because the sin of homosexuality is repulsive to most heterosexual people, many have reacted as if the people addicted to this sin are also repulsive. Some of us seem to have forgotten the biblical injunction to "speak the truth in love," so we have just spoken the truth, in tones that sound judgmental and unloving.

Stanton L. Jones wrote the fine piece I just alluded to. His article entitled "The Loving Opposition" appeared a few months ago in *Christianity Today*. Dr. Jones began his article talking about people he knows personally, people he genuinely likes, who are caught in the clutches of homosexual desire. He said he could not possibly address the issues involved without seeing their faces. This tempered his response, making him careful to speak clearly but lovingly so that his homosexual friends would hear in his words not only the truth about their behavior, but also the welcoming grace and love of Jesus.

For us to offer such a response to homosexuality is not easy. As Christians we have some basic convictions we cannot afford to cover up or deny. We have moral convictions that certain forms of behavior clearly are prohibited by our God and therefore are not permissible options for our lives. At the same time we have equally strong convictions that our God offers grace and healing to redeem us from all our sins. So, as Dr. Jones says in his article, "There are two things we must do. They are two things that do not naturally go together. We must exhibit the very love and compassion of Jesus Christ himself. And we must fearlessly proclaim the truth that Jesus Christ himself proclaimed and embodied."

Until now few Christians have spoken redemptively to people in the homosexual community. In my mind this is a tragedy. In an effort to extend grace and love to homosexuals, some Christian leaders have tried to explain away the fact that the Scriptures invariably condemn homosexual behavior. This is one approach that has been taken. It is not redemptive, in my opinion. It is permissive. On the other hand, Christians trying to affirm what the Bible says on the subject have virtually denied the Lord's love and grace for sinners. At least for homosexual sinners. This is not redemptive either.

So Lana's call that day stretched my wisdom and skill as a minister.

I like Lana, and she knows it. She's a fun-loving, intelligent, bubbly, creative, can-do kind of person. Nothing she said to me on the telephone changes that. We have laughed together and cried together through previous crises — crises that inevitably exposed some things about Lana she was not proud of at the time. But she knows that in spite of that knowledge I am still her friend. Back when the upheaval of her marriage had muddled her thinking, she would call me. Instead of rubber-stamping her mixed-up ideas, I tried to reflect truth and reality back at her. I think she appreciated it. I think that's one reason she kept calling. After all, isn't that what friends are for?

Now that Lana has fallen into a deeper delusion, can I still be a true friend if I tell her less than the truth? I doubt it.

I'm convinced now that Lana was testing all of this that last time she called. Will the love and grace she knows I preach still apply to her if I know she is living as a lesbian? Will almost four decades of friendship survive this revelation? Will that valued friendship cause me to compromise the moral demands of Scripture? Will it tempt me to violate my convictions and "bless the mess" Lana has chosen?

Lana probably knew the answer to those questions before she called me. But now that she has "come out," now that she has devastated her parents and her siblings with the heartbreaking announcement of her lesbian lifestyle and has forced them to make some sort of peace with a situation they can't stand but can't change, now she is testing her new identity on a broader circle of friends. Being able to make your friends' eyes widen while they gasp and search desperately for proper words to reply must surely give a person a strange new sense of being in control, not unlike the feedback a knock-out beauty gets when her entry into a crowded room draws all eyes and silences chatter momentarily. Lana would be an unusual person indeed if she was not secretly relishing her newfound power over people.

I sensed immediately that what I said to Lana during that phone call must be dictated by what she told me about her situation. Was she ashamed and tearfully seeking release from lesbianism? Was she reaching out for a hand to guide her out of an unspeakable mess? Or was she yearning for a hand to pat her on the head and affirm that she is a good little girl? Lana had to be the one to set the agenda for whatever conversation we would have that day. It was her call.

So I probed cautiously to find out where she was in her own mind. "How did your mom and dad react when you told them?" I queried. And I raised the same question about her sister and her brother. Maybe in her description of their reactions I could detect her own evaluation of herself. Finally I asked her point-blank, "Lana, are you comfortable with your situation right now?"

Without a flicker of hesitation she fired back, "I'm happier than I've ever been in my life. For the first time I feel free to be who I really am."

I began telling you about Lana by affirming that when we are broken, God will put us back together again. It's a glorious truth. But what if we don't think we're broken? What if we're convinced, like Lana, that we're O.K. when we're not? Then what can God do?

Everybody except Lana knows she is broken. Everybody, that is, except Lana and a few of her homosexual friends. By a complex process of rationalizing and denial and self-delusion they have convinced themselves that wrong is right. By redefining words and rewriting Scripture they have managed to turn nature on her head and have even convinced themselves that God approves of what they are doing. But everybody else knows Lana is broken.

Her parents know it. Who could begin to count the tears they have shed since she informed them of her sexual orientation? Because they are wise and loving parents who are unwilling to lose a daughter, they have stifled their anguish and horror. Deep down Lana probably knows better, but right now she chooses to interpret their kindness and love as approval. If only she could hear their prayers!

Lana's sister knows Lana is broken. When I asked

Lana how her family members were reacting to her homosexuality, she confessed to me, "Debbie had the hardest time accepting it." The truth is that Debbie knew she could speak her mind without losing her sister. So she told Lana the truth. She told her exactly what she thought of her decision to surrender to her lesbian impulses. Just how wrong and deviant she thought it was. Today Debbie doesn't say much. What else could she say? Lana, desperate to hang on to her family ties, misinterprets her sister's silence as acceptance.

The list of sensible, decent people who disapprove of Lana's lesbianism is long. Everybody in her family. Almost all of her former school friends. Most of the neighbors in her hometown, if they knew. The Christians she worshipped with as a child. To the list I would have to add myself, her pastoral counselor from afar. All of us who know Lana's choices grieve for her because we know the ruin and sorrow such a lifestyle must inevitably inflict upon her.

When the apostle Paul wrote to the Christians in the city of Corinth, he was ecstatic that some of his first converts had managed with God's help to free themselves from homosexual entanglements. "Such *were* some of you," Paul wrote. "But you were washed, you were sanctified, you were justified in the name of the Lord Jesus Christ and in the Spirit of our God." In Christ Paul's homosexual converts found healing for their brokenness. Redeemed and forgiven by the Lord Jesus, they left behind a degrading, destructive lifestyle and rejoiced that He made them able to live wholesome, healthy lives by His power.

I'm sure the Lord could do the same thing for Lana. But through the ages God has placed one restriction on his grace: He never will force his blessings upon us against our will. Patiently the Almighty waits for Lana to say to him, "Thy will be done." But if she refuses, if she adamantly insists that nothing is wrong with the way she is living, then God will sorrowfully say to Lana, "*Your* will be done." And he will give her up to the brokenness she has chosen.

The Pharisees' Leaven

When so many thousands of the multitude had gathered together that they trod upon one another, he began to say to his disciples first, "Beware of the leaven of the Pharisees, which is hypocrisy. Nothing is covered up that will not be revealed, or hidden that will not be known. Therefore whatever you have said in the dark shall be heard in the light, and what you have whispered in private rooms shall be proclaimed upon the housetops. I tell you, my friends, do not fear those who kill the body, and after that have no more that they can do. But I will warn you whom to fear: fear him who, after he has killed, has power to cast into hell; yes, I tell you, fear him! Are not five sparrows sold for two pennies? And not one of them is forgotten before God. Why, even the hairs of your head are all numbered. Fear not; you are of more value than many sparrows. And I tell you, every one who acknowledges me before men, the Son of man also will acknowledge before the angels of God; but he who denies me before men will be denied before the angels of God. And every one who speaks a word against the Son of man will be forgiven; but he who blasphemes against the Holy Spirit will not be forgiven. And when they bring you before the synagogues and the rulers and the authorities, do not be anxious how or what you are to answer or what you are to say; for the Holy Spirit will teach you in that very hour what you ought to say" (Luke 12:1-12).

My first car was a 1941 Studebaker.

Jet-black, four doors (that opened on each side like the double doors of a house, with the hinges on the far left and the far right and opening in the middle). With the original upholstery still spotless when I became its proud owner in the mid-Fifties and with its black exterior glistening like luminous ebony, that jalopy was a thing of beauty.

Even by the time I bought it that model of Studebaker was nearly extinct. None of my school buddies had ever seen one. So when I came puttering up to high school in mine on the first day of my sophomore year (back when all but a handful of the cars on the road were made in Detroit by Americans), all the kids thought I had an expensive, exotic foreign car.

Most of the time I babied that old car. No hotrodding (the clouds of oil smoke belching out the tailpipe warned against wrapping up its six cylinders very tight). No rubber-peeling starts (did Studebaker ever make a car that would peel out?). No drag-racing or ditching or daredevil stunts in that car. When a fellow spent the hours I spent washing and polishing and currying a vehicle, he wasn't about to go out and mess it up acting dumb.

But one warm fall night my mother-hen pride in that classic Studebaker gave way to a much more basic human drive. With a sardine-can load of church kids aboard I came barreling home on the deserted road from Palo Duro Canyon, and I was showing off for my passengers.

Before that night I doubt the old jitney had run more than 50 miles per hour in years, but that night the speedometer needle was pegged. It took a long way to get that tiny flathead engine up to that kind of speed, and to my horror I found out that it took almost that far to get it stopped again.

We were mindlessly flying toward the city lights when we topped a rise in the road and suddenly, not half a mile ahead, the highway was filled with flashing lights and scrunched-up cars and patrolmen and people milling around an accident scene.

Desperately I began to pump the brakes on that Studebaker, brakes that were not good enough even to slide the tires. I stood up on them and almost pulled the steering wheel off, trying vainly to hold back my carload of humanity as we hurtled through the dark toward the unsuspecting ant bed of activity in the road ahead.

"We're going to hit them," I thought. "These old brakes will never stop us." But they did. We oozed at least a dozen feet past the signalling highway patrol-man and finally stopped rolling not ten yards from the wreck already piled up in front of us.

It took me a long time that night to stop the shaking inside me, and it has taken much longer than that for me to forget how near I came to causing a massive tragedy because I let a crowd of observers tempt me to show off.

The Roar of the Crowd

Isn't that why we usually show off? Because some-body is watching us? Surely it was not just a coinci-dence that Jesus warned his men about the danger of religious pretending right at a time when a large crowd had gathered.

Luke, who was always so careful of details in his history, begins Chapter 12 by telling us that "so many thousands of the multitude had gathered together that they trod upon one another." That's quite a crowd — when people are stepping on each other!

And it was precisely in that setting — when Jesus and his men were surrounded by hordes of people — that our Lord thought it necessary to caution his men about showing off. "Beware of the leaven of the Pharisees," he warned. Then the Master quickly explained in plainer language that he wanted his men to avoid hypocrisy.

The Living Bible helps me here. In Verse 1 we hear Jesus saying to his disciples, "Beware of these Pharisees and the way they pretend to be good when they aren't." Isn't that the essence of hypocrisy: pretending to be something we are not? Jesus seems to have been afraid that the presence of so many onlookers might tempt his men to show off their spiritual insights and gifts.

Evidently the leading Pharisees liked to "strut their stuff" before their followers, impressing them with their mastery of obscure Bible texts and their gnat's-eyelash command of complicated Jewish rituals. Before their people on the Sabbath they put on a "religious" face and pretended a piety unseen in their actual day-to-day dealings. They were hypocrites who played to the crowd.

"Beware of that kind of duplicity," Jesus cautioned. It is a cancer that eats the guts out of true religion. All of us who are active in our religion, and especially those of us who are called to lead in public worship need to listen closely to our Lord's warning.

Nobody is tempted to pretend in private. We show off only when we have an audience. Hypocrisy is a group activity.

A Tough Guy

A friend of mine told me recently about a scary encounter that demonstrates what I'm talking about.

As a state social worker my friend drew the dubious task of protecting a battered family from the husband and father, who was a hardened motorcycle gang leader. Around his gang members this almost-forty-year-old thug swaggered and swore and flexed his arm-length tattoos, trying to prove how tough he was. Flanked by his fellow-thugs, he was a macho man who boasted of the muggings and murders he had instigated.

This long-haired, grizzled biker came to the welfare office with chains clanking from his big belt and with a huge knife tucked conspicuously under it. But the macho exterior crumbled when my social worker friend in a business suit, a genteel man half the thug's size, looked him squarely in the eye and told him exactly how state law protected his abused family from him.

Alone, with no buddies on Harleys to back up his boasts, this macho biker cowered and whined. As my friend recalled the event, he chuckled and told me, "The big, bad thug turned out to be a wimp."

At least this much church folks and Hell's Angels have in common: the pride that makes us pretend to be something we're not is triggered by an audience. The sin of hypocrisy is activated in us only when we think somebody else is watching.

A teenage driver stupidly speeds down a dark country road in an old Studebaker only when the car is full of other teens whom he needs to impress.

Gang leaders spout tough-guy talk only when the gang is there to listen.

Apostles are tempted to flaunt their eloquence or to display flamboyant miracles only when a curious crowd is present to ooh and ah.

Jesus understood this. He knew the power a crowd to prompt our pride and to unleash deep within us the carnal craving to have others think we're better than we really are. So, when the crowd drew near, he warned his men, "Beware of hypocrisy." In our crowded churches today we need to hear his warning.

Wasted Effort

In those early verses of Luke 12 Jesus has a second truth to tell us about religious pretending. Not only is such hypocrisy stirred up by an audience, but Jesus also wants us to see that the considerable energy we expend to maintain a pretense is almost always wasted.

"Nothing is covered up that will not be revealed," Jesus points out. "Nothing is hidden that will not be known." Our most elaborate pretenses will not hide our imperfections and our brokenness. Not from God. Nor from our neighbors.

The long prayers prayed on the street corners in Jerusalem did not really convince anybody that the pray-er was particularly pious. In most cases they probably made the performer look foolish, even as overly-long prayers do today.

The contributions pretentiously plunked into the temple treasury before an audience drawn by trumpets heralding the event did not really make anybody think that the rich man loved either God or the poor. The onlookers always left convinced that the rich man loved himself. Religious pretense always leads to that conclusion about the pretender.

In other words, our efforts to look better than we are almost always accomplish the very opposite. People smell our hypocrisy and go away suspecting that we must have something to hide. As a result of our pretenses, other people think worse of us, not better.

Besides that, Jesus wants us to realize, you can't hide anything anyway. "Whatever you have said in the dark shall be heard in the light, and what you have whispered in private rooms shall be proclaimed upon the housetops."

If you doubt that truth, talk to Richard Nixon about his tapes. Talk to Bill Clinton about Whitewater.

Our wrong actions and wicked words have a frightening way of surfacing at just the wrong time. Sins we thought nobody could possibly know about have a scary way of becoming public knowledge.

Do you remember Ananias and Sapphira? They were so sure their scheme would work. How could anyone in the church possibly know the selling price of that field? In secret they plotted. "We'll tuck away a few thousand for our own use," they agreed, "but to keep from looking stingy alongside folks like Barnabas, we'll make it look like we're donating the whole wad."

They were so greedy for praise.

They were so sure their lie would go undetected.

In fact, they were dead sure.

Today the church is safer, we think. Peter is long dead. We no longer have apostles lurking in the church foyer miraculously discerning our deceptions. God has not given any preacher I know the power to strike you dead if you're a hypocrite. The day of Ananias and Sapphira is long past. Right?

Wrong. Most folks don't need miraculous powers to

tell when our religion is fake. If my faith and hope and love are counterfeit, all the pretense and hypocrisy I can muster won't hide it.

If I smile and shake your hand, when in fact I disdain or resent you, you'll know it.

If I loudly profess that the church is the most important aspect of my life, and then somehow I am never available when the members assemble or when the work takes place, do you think I'll fool anybody?

If one day a week I sing praises like an angel, and then all week long I treat my family like the devil, do you think my wife and kids will buy my act?

Bitterness and greed are like crayon marks on a bedroom wall. Paint over them and they bleed right back through. Envy and anger and lust and hate are so indelibly etched on our faces that all the whitewash in the world will not hide them from view. Only the blood of Jesus applied with genuine penitence can cover the sins that blotch our souls.

Holy Openness

Most of us are familiar with the teachings of Jesus in Luke 12 immediately following his warnings about hypocrisy. Usually, though, we have heard the verses quoted one or two at time in isolated snatches and thus we may have failed to hear the compelling logic of our Lord in verses 4-12.

In the first verses of Luke 12 we have heard Jesus warning us about trying to pretend to be better than we really are, and we have heard him telling us how impossible it would be for us to hide anything we might be ashamed of. Now, moving from a negative tone of cautioning to a more positive vein of exhortation, Jesus counsels us to be set free from fear by the confident, open confession of our faith.

We worship a God who knows everything, Jesus reasons. Our God keeps track of the tiniest sparrows flitting through a jillion obscure corners of the earth. He numbers the hairs that drop almost unseen from your head.

In other words, not even the most insignificant happenings on this globe escape God's attention. And Jesus insists that you and I are not insignificant. A God who keeps track of sparrows and hairs will certainly know what is going on in our lives.

If we are sad, He knows it.

If we are mad, He knows it.

If we are loving, or lazy, or happy, or heartbroken, the God of heaven knows what is happening in our hearts.

It behooves us then to be totally open and above board in the practice of our faith. "Everyone who acknowledges me before men," Jesus promises, "the Son of man will acknowledge before the angels of God."

Thus the argument of Jesus comes full circle. Instead of being the sort of religious people who are always pretending goodness and hiding their true nature, Jesus calls us to be men and women who confidently and openly confess our faith in him. The result can be freedom from anxiety and fear.

"Fear Not!"

The person who is hiding something is always afraid. A fellow with a guilty conscience is always running from something that isn't chasing him.

Is that why Jesus keeps talking about fear as he teaches us in Luke 12 about hypocrisy and openness? If we accept his call to live open and transparent lives among his people, he assures us that we can unload much of our fear.

Some wiseman has counselled young preachers to quickly confess their faults and weaknesses to their new congregations. Thus, this sage observed, they will take away from potential opponents any ammunition that might have been used against them.

Even in the face of extreme opposition, Jesus says, we do not have to be afraid if we have been open and true in our confession of him. "Do not be anxious how or what you are to answer, or what you are to say," Jesus advises all who are under attack for their faith. And he promises, "The Holy Spirit will teach you in that very hour what you ought to say."

Have you experienced that kind of heavenly help? I have. And I must confess to you that it still amazes me when the Spirit comes so quickly and so visibly to my aid. Is that a weakness of belief on my part, that I should be surprised when the Lord does exactly what he said he would do for me?

I am convinced that if I would more fully trust Jesus' promises in these verses of Luke 12, then I could more fully share in the comfort he offers in these verses; for he plainly says, "Do not be anxious. Fear not."

Lifestyle Faith

Out on that country road in my old Studebaker, the teachings of Jesus in Luke 12 were the farthest thing from my mind.

There I was, in a potentially disastrous mess, that

could have been avoided if I had been obeying Jesus' counsel in this chapter. (It does occur to me that tragedy may have been averted that night because the God who watches over sparrows also takes care of young idiots in worn-out Studebakers. If that is true, then Luke 12 had more to do with that night than I realized at the time.)

But the point I'm trying to make is that the wisdom of Jesus' teaching in this chapter can't help us much if we wait until we're already flying down the road in the Studebaker to remember it.

When we have already surrendered to the roar of the crowd, and our deception and hypocrisy already have us in a jam, it's too late to claim the promises of Luke 12.

We can calm our anxieties and tame our fears only if we begin in the less pressured moments of our lives to practice the honesty and openness Jesus calls us to, and to establish these qualities as the way we always conduct our lives. Then we're ready for the Studebaker.

Then the opinions of people around us can't push us into stupid pretenses that compromise our faith and jeopardize our integrity.

Then our confession will hold firm and people will know that we are real.

Dignity Restored

"Ask, and it will be given you; seek, and you will find; knock, and it will be opened to you" (Matthew 7:7).

Has your prayer been answered if you ask for health and God instead gives you patience to bear your pain? If in weakness you beg for strength, and God instead sends a brother or sister to carry your load, has He granted your request?

I wonder how many prayers Annie Hisel had prayed. I wonder how many times she had wept shamelessly before God, pleading for Him to restore the dignity she had known before multiple sclerosis turned her legs into useless toothpicks and made her hands forget how to find her mouth to wipe away the moisture that dribbled unbidden from lips she no longer could keep closed. I wonder how many times Annie screamed for God to release her from her unthinkable wretchedness.

God knows, Annie had more than enough time to pray such prayers. Day after day Annie sat in her squalid home, strapped into a straight-backed chair to keep her from falling into a helpless heap on the floor. For ten hours every day, while her unmarried school-teacher daughter was away in her classroom, Annie sat captive in that abominable chair. With no water. No food. No sanitary facilities but the hole cut in her chair bottom and the rank-smelling bucket beneath. She sat there hour after hour in that awful stench, with nothing more to do than to mouth garbled instructions to the canary that flew loose throughout the house, and to the multiple cats who also roamed the premises.

Annie and her daughter lived frugally. They had no TV. In the early days Annie passed her lonely hours reading. But now her frozen fingers would not turn the pages and her disobedient muscles refused to hold a book. Before long any magazine or novel her daughter left on her baby-chair-like tray would soon be swept into the floor by the jerk of a wayward arm, and it would lie there less than a yard from her feet. By its very presence all day long it would mock her inability to reach down and pick it up. So Annie gave up reading.

Occasionally a benevolent neighbor stopped in to say hi, but most of them got one good whiff of the odor inside the front door and made their visits few and brief.

"When you're out making calls," one of our church members begged me, "stop by to see Annie Hisel." She wrote down Annie's address on a slip of paper. "Rap on the door and she'll answer you. Then just go on in," my friend explained. "She can't get up to open the door for you."

Getting Past the Smell

That's how I met Annie. One Tuesday morning about 11:15 I located the address and let myself into the strange house just as I had been instructed. At once my nose was assaulted by the acrid odor of human and animal urine, a smell I had initially encountered in the worst of the primitive nursing homes I visited during my first years of student preaching. I hated that smell then. I didn't like it any better now. When I stepped inside, I saw Annie, ensconced on her humiliating throne, queen of her pigsty. She smiled, as nearly as her advanced M.S. would let her, and graciously welcomed me into her home with syllables unlike any language my ears had ever heard before.

"Mrs. Hisel?" I inquired. A flurry of nods confirmed that I had the right lady.

"Your neighbor Ellie attends the church where I preach," I told her. "She asked me to stop by to see you. She told me you weren't able to get out and around very much anymore."

Annie beamed a smile that looked more like a grimace. She didn't get much company. Even the presence of a bumbling young preacher from a church she had never heard of was better than an empty house. I learned later that she had tolerated lengthy tutoring sessions by Jehovah's Witness teachers with whom she totally disagreed. She put up with them just to have another human being in the house.

I wasn't sure I could stay in the place. With a nod of

her head (the only muscular movement Annie still seemed able to control halfway dependably) and with a wild gesture of an unruly hand, Annie indicated that I should make myself comfortable on the divan or on the huge stuffed chair beside it. A quick glance convinced me that I would be forever blighted if I lit on either. Bird droppings from the dive-bombing canary adorned both pieces of furniture. What the bird missed, the cats covered with hair — and worse. I guess you could say they were housebroken. The bird and the cats. If by "housebroken" you meant that they never went anywhere except in the house. The entire Hisel residence was their litter box. I found a kitchen chair which had been somewhat protected by its position under the table's edge and dared to perch on it for the hardest 20-minute visit in my entire preaching career.

"I'll try to get by to see you again soon, Mrs. Hisel," I told her as I left, but everything inside me wanted out of that house. Away from that smell. Out of that filth.

Still, in the days that followed I couldn't forget Annie Hisel. I could get up and walk away from that mess, but she couldn't. By forces she could not control and by a fate she had no say in, she was trapped in that horrid house. Worse than that she was confined in a virtually useless body. Imprisonment for Annie included being part of a family who never meant to abuse or neglect her but who seemed for some reason to lack the simple social awareness of how to do any better. At first, she told me, her retired carpenter husband had cared for her, arranging his daily duties so that he could attend to her needs at least hourly. When he died suddenly, Annie begged her son and daughter, "Don't put me in a nursing home." So they honored her wishes. After the funeral the son went home half a continent away. The daughter stayed at home and did the best for mama she knew how to do. And it was awful.

How Annie managed to tolerate those wretched days I'll never know. Surely there must have been days when she wished fervently for somebody like Jack Kevorkian. Days when she screamed with Job, "Why, God, did you let me be born?"

For Better, For Worse

Someone has said that the greatest difference between people is not whether they are black or white. Rich or poor. Educated or uneducated. The greatest difference may be between those of us who have good health and those who don't.

When we're young, most of us don't think much about this. At least, I know I didn't. With strong, fit bodies, we go blithely about our business, seldom hampered by weakness or pain. We eat what we please. We tackle any task. We burn the candle at both ends, never once imagining that our bodies might someday be unable to perform such duties or to keep up the pace.

Is any blessing less appreciated than good health while we have it? Few blessings are more yearned for than good health when we have forever lost it.

Annie Hisel was probably like the rest of us. She never expected to be in such distasteful circumstances. I learned that Annie grew up in a financially comfortable home. Born to parents who came from the old country and who worked tirelessly to guarantee America's economic blessings for their children, Annie and her two brothers enjoyed the advantages of culture and refinement. Music lessons. Good books. Private schooling. Not to mention such basics as warm clothing and good food and comfortable housing. Her parents would have been horrified had they lived to see Annie's plight after M.S. did its dreadful work on her. In her worst nightmares I doubt that Annie ever dreamed she would end up like she was the day I met her. Blessed with a sharp mind and a strong body, in her healthy days Annie had infused her home with good humor and with a robust spirit. Like Job on the day before his disasters, in the days before M.S. Annie would probably have told you that life just couldn't get much better. But, as Job found out to his horror, it could get worse. Much worse. For Job. For Annie. For you, or me.

Today's health, and wealth, and present security are no guarantee for tomorrow. Reality admonishes us to savor the good days. They may not last.

Annie's Blessing

I kept my promise to Annie. Back to that stinking house I returned. For several months, at least once a week I held her hand and read to her from the Scriptures. Sensing her desperate need for companionship, I convinced the ladies at our church to move their Wednesday morning Bible study to Annie's living room. Such a move was impossible, of course, until the place was cleaned up. So a handful of our stalwart gals held their noses and stifled their gagging while they scrubbed and fumigated the place. To keep the house usable, we persuaded Annie and her daughter to give away some of the animal residents and to restrict the movement of the others. We found a visiting nurse and a social worker who offered valuable advice and assistance in upgrading Annie's personal care. Despite our best efforts the place still reeked, but not like it did before our ladies worked their magic.

After transforming Annie's house, a couple of our ladies went to work on Annie herself. Once a week they spent the morning bathing her and washing her long neglected hair. Annie glowed with new self-respect and happiness the first time I saw her after these ablutions. More important than Annie's new smell, however, were the new friendships that were emerging. Whether we came to study Scriptures or to scrub floors, all of us found ourselves falling in love with Annie. Once we got past the smell and quit being horrified by her physical impairments, we came to know the real Annie. And we liked her. She was a grand lady, with a wealth of memories to share and with a head full of present ideas to express — now that she had someone besides the bird or the cats to listen to her. We soon learned to decipher Annie's slurred dialect, with one or the other of us often interpreting for the rest of the group. Annie would smile and nod vigorously to let us know when the interpreter got it right.

In Annie we found something more than an interesting lady. In her we found a heart full of courage and faith. She had survived her most dismal days by affirming with the apostle Paul that "the sufferings of this present time are not worth comparing to the glory that is to be revealed to us." Instead of giving up and cursing life as a person without faith might have done, Annie joined the generations of Christians before her who, instead of becoming bitter, embraced their trials as a way to become better, saying, "We rejoice in our sufferings, knowing that suffering produces endurance, and endurance produces character, and character produces hope, and hope does not disappoint us, because God's love has been poured into our hearts through the Holy Spirit which has been given to us" (Romans 5:3-5). Like the great apostle, Annie had learned to be content in whatever condition she found herself. In health or in sickness, in strength or in weakness, in dignity or in humiliation, Annie focused not on what she had lost, but on what she still had, and thanked God for it. Her quiet contentment shamed our discontent and silenced our own complaints.

No doubt about it. God used Annie to bless us. But it's equally true that He used us to bless her, too. Both physically and mentally Annie seemed to blossom as her new Christian friends ministered to her. Alone all day, strapped in that horrid chair, Annie had long ago abandoned any hope of therapy for her atrophied muscles. Led by a visiting nurse, our ladies consulted with a physical therapist and began exercising Annie's neglected limbs. Much of her poor coordination turned out to be the result of weakness. Soon our ladies had Annie feeding herself again and even brushing her own hair. Ever since Annie stopped reading months before, she had allowed her mind to wander aimlessly for hours at a time. Now she was mentally focused again, holding conversations that challenged and entertained her more than those she had conducted with the bird and the cats. Having almost vegetated in her seemingly hopeless mess, Annie came alive again. Week by week I watched her progress with amazement and delight.

An Annie Near You

"Bear one another's burdens," the Scriptures instruct us, "and so fulfill the law of Christ." This is the ultimate will of Him who "came not to be served, but to serve." As He gave Himself for us, so He wills that we give up ourselves to lift up others.

Years ago, while interviewing Dr. Karl Menninger, a young reporter asked, "Dr. Menninger, if you thought you were about to have a nervous breakdown, what would you do?" He expected the famous psychiatrist to recommend a quick consultation with some sort of mental health professional. But Dr. Menninger surprised him. "Young man," he answered, "if I thought I was about to have a mental breakdown, I would immediately leave my house, lock my door, and go across the street and look for some way to help another person."

Although Annie entered our church building only once in more than a decade, she blessed our entire congregation. God used her to call us outside of ourselves and to teach us the timeless truth that real happiness comes from what we give and not from what we get.

In a very real sense God worked through that little church to answer Annie's prayers. When hope was gone, when life was unlivable, when each day had become a ordeal to endure, God used that band of selfless Christian women to bring life and love and laughter back into Annie's world.

Is there an Annie nearby who needs you?

Life in Unit B

"For God hath not given us the spirit of fear; but of power, and of love, and of a sound mind" (2 Timothy 1:7, KJV).

"After you have suffered a little while," the Scriptures promise us, "the God of all grace . . . will himself restore, establish, and strengthen you." Literally, the promise is that the Lord will mend our broken bones. He will put us back together again.

In our world there are many forms of human brokenness.

Even a short list would include bankruptcies, divorces, imprisonments, lost health, and terminal illnesses. Blindness, lost hearing, and physical handicaps of all sorts would surely belong on the inventory. I would include on the list anything that can break our hearts and crush our spirits. At the top of my list, though, leading my catalog of human brokenness, I would place severe mental illness.

Go with me for a moment into the world of insanity. Feel with me its hurt and horror.

My visit to Unit B that day made my skin crawl.

As I drove out the gates of the state mental hospital and merged with the work hour traffic headed back into town, my mind was a muddle. My adrenalin was still pumping. Conflicting feelings of fear and sympathy and excitement and relief overloaded my circuits and blocked any clear analysis of the experience I had just completed.

"I would like to visit with Elsie Jackson," I had told the guard at the hospital gate, identifying myself as a local minister.

He ran his forefinger down the roster of patients. "You'll find her in Unit B," he said as he handed me a visitor's pass to display on my car's windshield. "Have you visited there before?" he asked.

No. I had not visited Unit B ever in my life. So the little man gave me careful instructions to guide me through the unfamiliar maze of narrow streets on the state hospital grounds. "The door to Unit B will be locked," he told me. "Press the buzzer and someone will let you in."

The Road to Unit B

As I slowly made my way westward between the rambling assortment of shabby stucco buildings, I wondered what I was about to get into. At church the Sunday before Elsie's mother and brother had asked me if I would be willing to visit her. Having just moved to town, with less than six weeks of that ministry under my belt, I had no idea who Elsie was. No details about her sickness. No knowledge of the years of anguish she and her family had been through.

"Elsie's been at the State Hospital for about six months this time," they told me. "She doesn't get much company. They only let the family visit on Saturday afternoons, and we can't always make it then. They stopped letting her attend the chapel services at the hospital. Your visits would mean a lot to her." I agreed to drop in on Elsie.

Few things in our society have changed as much in the past four decades as the way we go about caring for those who are mentally ill.

The hospital where Elsie resided was perched on the brink of monumental changes. They were just about to shift from treatment modes adopted in places like Bedlam in the 1800's to more enlightened therapies of the modern age. But, when I came to visit that day, they had not made those changes yet. Most of the buildings were ancient. Beyond hope of adequate repair. If you were time-warped back to that hospital campus on that day, you would probably think you had splashed down in some third world country. An inferior one, at that. As I wound my way toward Unit B, I had no idea what awaited me there.

Out on the grassy areas along the road several dozen patients were enjoying the sunshine and the first hints of fall weather. At first you might have mistaken it for a city park. At least until one of the more disturbed patients turned and leered at you as you drove by. It did not take long for me to see that these folks roaming the grounds inside the high wrought-iron fences were not your everyday, normal neighbors. They were very sick people who would not fare well on the other side of those fences. I suppose some of them resented the fences and wished they weren't there. But for most of these folks the impenetrable barriers were a welcome guarantee of security. Like babies in a playpen, the patients inside these fences were protected from outside dangers they could not cope with and from inner impulses they could not control. One middle-aged couple, both of them seriously retarded, sat smooching on a park bench in front of God and everybody. They were in love, and didn't care who knew it.

After a wrong turn or two, I found Unit B. In the months that followed I would learn that it was commonly referred to by the staff and patients alike as "the lock-up ward." Unit B housed the patients who were dangerous to themselves and to others. Elsie Jackson was a patient in Unit B.

Meeting Elsie

As I had been instructed, I pressed the button beside the door and heard a raspy buzzer resonating somewhere deep in the bowels of that awful place. Presently an orderly in a white uniform appeared, read my pass for the longest time, and then let me enter. As soon as I stepped inside, the orderly turned his keys in three locks on the door. I was now locked inside with whatever craziness infested this place. Which turned out to be more than I ever could have imagined.

"Wait here," the orderly instructed me. "I'll go find Elsie for you."

So I waited, in a tiny foyer that contained a miniature sofa and a dilapidated stuffed chair. From where I sat I could see into the semi-darkness of a large commons area. It was an empty room perhaps 35 feet wide and 60 feet long, without a stick of furniture in it. Around its perimeter people were shuffling along. Or standing as if ready to walk. Several stood like frozen statues, textbook cases of catatonic paralysis. Many of the wretched band were in varied states of undress, some totally nude. Hospital personnel long ago had accepted the fact that nobody could keep clothes on them. One naked old lady, severely stooped by age or maybe by injury, trudged non-stop around the edge of the room. During my visit she crossed my line of vision five or six times. From farther back in the unknown recesses of Unit B came occasional shrieks and moans. Unearthly sounds from pitiful creatures who were restrained for their own protection. Here I was in an almost medieval insane asylum, before the advent of most psycho-therapeutic drugs, in a time when chains and locks and bars were still the only way to control the uncontrollable. I felt as if I had stumbled into some hideous anteroom in Dante's hell.

"Hi!" a mannish, broad-bodied woman with a wider-than-normal smile breezily greeted me. It was Elsie. I was glad to see that she was one of the patients who kept their clothes on. In fact, she was rather neatly dressed. In a clean starched white pinafore crisscrossed with row upon row of tiny blue flowers. Her slightly graying hair was braided tightly atop her head. Two or three missing front teeth broadened her unnatural grin.

Elsie sat in the tattered old chair, fidgeting while I introduced myself. Instantly she accepted me into her weird world like a long-lost friend. And we chit-chatted for quite awhile about the few things we knew we had in common. Her mother. Yes, I knew her mother. Yes, Mom was just fine when I saw her Sunday. And, yes, Elsie's brother had finished patching Mom's roof that leaked the last time it rained. No, I had never met Elsie's kids. How many did she have? Three. Where were they? Off in another state with their father. But they would come to see her when school was out. She was sure of that.

Most of the conversation was lucid. At least her part was. When we touched on certain subjects, though, Elsie would get suddenly agitated. She would begin to stutter, or fall silent. Then, as if someone inside her had flipped a switch, she would flash that exaggerated, toothy grin and take off on a totally different subject. Her trolley swapped tracks quite often, with ease. Part of the time I'm not sure it was on a track.

I was not unhappy when the orderly with the keys to that kingdom reappeared. It gave me a cue to say goodbye. Elsie cheerily thanked me for coming and asked me if I would come back tomorrow. Well, not tomorrow. But I would come back, I promised.

And I did. Unit B became a regular stop on my weekly pastoral rounds. And Elsie became my friend.

*****

"It took twelve men to put me to bed last night," Elsie giggled one afternoon, with a crazy glint dancing in her eyes. She was wilder that day than I had seen her before.

"Twelve men!?" I exclaimed.

"That's right," she blustered. And then with a maniacal laugh she proudly explained, "I set fire to the trash can while I was smoking, and it took twelve of them to put out the fire and get me into the straightjacket and tie me onto the bed." She seemed downright pleased with herself.

By now I had heard Elsie's mother's tale about the previous summer when the hospital had sent Elsie home on leave. At first Elsie had been fine. A bit at loose ends. Nervous. And easily angered. But for the most part Elsie had controlled herself. Until the third week when Elsie's mother spotted the tell-tale signs of Elsie's insanity returning. "I hid the butcher knife that afternoon," she told me, "and I stayed awake all night long for fear that Elsie would go berserk and kill us all." The next day they had taken Elsie back to the hospital.

I thought of this as Elsie boasted of her superhuman strength. I thought, too, of the wild man in Mark's Gospel, who broke chains when the neighbors tried to restrain him. I wondered what I would do if Elsie came unhinged and turned that muscle loose on me. Sadly I wondered if Elsie had days when she was not proud of her brawn. Days when she was terrified of her own destructive potential. Days when she was ashamed to be a psychotic threat to the people who loved her.

Elsie was elated when they let her out of Unit B. I'll never forget her excitement. In girlish patter, and with smiles no longer so overdone, she announced to me one day that our next visit would be in an adjacent dorm. Or, if we wanted to, we could go outside and visit on the bench under the trees, because she wouldn't be locked up anymore. She was ecstatic. This new freedom put her one step closer to going home to her mother's. One step nearer to being able to care for her own children. This was my first solid clue that Elsie was getting better. She had stopped bragging about her crazy behavior and began to dream out loud about being sane and whole again.

No Right Answers

That day when I first met Elsie Jackson was over thirty years ago. Improvements in health care for the mentally ill have come light-years since then. Dingy, smelly, inhuman asylums have been replaced in civilized countries by modern, clean, comfortable facilities. New behavior-modifying drugs help to control behavior and make normal life possible for some who would have been permanently institutionalized only a few decades ago. In recent months controlled studies of treatment with a new drug called Clozaril have given schizophrenic patients what some of them call "miraculous" release from the symptoms of their illness.

Despite these victories, however, mental illness remains one of the most tragic forms of human brokenness. Loved ones of those with serious mental problems face struggles the rest of us cannot imagine. And the mentally ill themselves contend constantly with handicaps and frustrations beyond our comprehension.

Last week I visited with a mother whose 35-year-old daughter requires almost constant care because of recurring bouts of schizophrenia. The fact that this mother is wealthy and socially prominent does not exempt her from the tears and turbulence that go with this disease. Lovingly she does the best she can to bring some order into the life of her daughter's child. But her heart aches as she sees her grandchild buffeted and bruised by the unpredictable behavior of a mentally ill mother. "Every day is a new challenge," this good lady told me, trying to smile. Then as a tear slipped down her cheek, she confessed, "For what we're dealing with, there are no right answers." I agreed.

My own brilliant sister graduated from a major university with a 4-point grade average. She has an I.Q. over 140. She has received the highest possible evaluations on every job she has ever held. But time and again through the years she has lost good jobs, and today she is unemployed, because mental illness continues to rear its head.

I visited last month with the Christian mother of a young man who borrowed a preacher's rifle one morning and, sniping from atop a downtown motel, shot seven strangers to death before police subdued him. She will never understand what went haywire in her baby's brain to make him do that. Last year her husband went to an early grave grieving over the mental illness of their child, who will likely spend the rest of his days behind bars.

Good News for the Afflicted

"The Spirit of the Lord God is upon me," Jesus proclaimed, "because the Lord has anointed me to bring good tidings to the afflicted; he has sent me to bind up the brokenhearted." The Psalmist sang, "The Lord is near to the brokenhearted, and saves the crushed in spirit." Without such promises to bolster our spirits, unsolvable sorrows such as mental illness would be impossible to bear.

"Bear one another's burdens," we are commanded as followers of Christ. When we do so, the Scriptures assure us, we "fulfill the law of Christ." Jesus bids us to "weep with those who weep." And we must obey, for it will be hard for our loved ones to make it through the dark days of mental illness even with our support and our understanding and our love.

Elsie Jackson's family handled her problems wisely. Resisting the natural impulse to suffer silently because of embarrassment and needless shame, they shared their fears and concerns with Christians who loved them. At first I think they were a bit surprised to see that their openness about Elsie's troubles caused their friends to love them more, not less. In the company of caring believers they found help and healing for their hurting hearts.

Thus, in a situation that seemed so bleak, Elsie's family discovered through personal experience that Peter knew what he was talking about. "After you have suffered a little while," Peter promised, "the God of all grace, who has called you to his eternal glory in Christ, will himself restore, establish, and strengthen you." He'll put us back together again.

The Sin Unto Death

"Since they did not see fit to acknowledge God, God gave them up to a base mind and to improper conduct"(Romans 1:28).

"There is a sin unto death," the apostle John says at the end of his first letter. Some people are so bad for so long that they wind up beyond the reach of their mothers' prayers. Beyond the sound of Eternal Truth. Beyond the redemptive love of the One who died for them. Stooping to do evil again and again, these habitual sinners become spiritual hunchbacks with crippled consciences and withered wills. Long ago their spirits have lost the moral strength to stand upright. It does no good to call such people to goodness. They have chosen to be deaf. If we could transport them miraculously into the very heart of Heaven, they would be even more miserable than they are now on the rare occasions when we force them to associate with the church, for they have lost all taste for heavenly things.

Concerning such people the Bible says more than once, "God gave them up." What an absolutely awful description to apply to any human being! This is the God who forgave David when he murdered Uriah and stole his wife. This is the God who told the adulteress, "I don't condemn you," and then gave her another chance. This is the God who had room in heaven for a crucified thief and prayed that his own murderers might be forgiven for their sin. This God, so full of mercy and grace — this God who says he does not want a single person to perish — still encounters some individuals so vile, so evil, so sold on sin, that he gives up on them and lets them go their own wicked way. A way that leads inevitably to ruin. Let me tell you a story about a fellow like that. It's a true story, with only the names and a few details changed out of respect for people I love.

✳ ✳ ✳ ✳ ✳

Ken Williams (that's what I'll call him) was one of the sharpest, most promising young men I ever met. Today he is behind bars. And all of us who know him — even his own mother — hope he stays there.

Ken was a sophomore in high school when I met him. Like his two older brothers before him, he came out of puberty looking like some sort of Greek god. His mama worshipped him, as did the adolescent females in that small Arkansas town, who clustered about him and swooned when he so much as glanced at them.

Handsome to a fault, smarter than any kid ought to be, Ken appeared at first to be a model child. When I came to preach summer revivals at the village church where his parents worshipped, I usually bunked at Ken's home, so I got a close-up look at the way Ken and his siblings got along with each other and with their parents. Mama could hardly conceal her conviction that each of her offspring was a cut above other folks' sons and daughters. Aside from this, I saw not a hint that this family was headed for big-time troubles. Mama was clearly the dominant personality in the house. Uncomfortably so at times. But she probably had to be, I figured, since Ken's father was such a quiet, compliant soul. After I spent my first week in their home, my gut-level assessment of this family was that they were decent, extremely hard-working, God-fearing people. I liked them. Especially I liked Ken.

Veteran West Texas fishermen will understand what I mean when I tell you that Ken was the only fellow who ever offered me a chance to telephone a catfish. (Yankees and others may need me to explain that if you take the bare ends of wires hooked up to an old crank telephone, drop them into a fishing hole, and crank hard, catfish in that hole will be so shocked that they float to the surface belly-up. Local game wardens take a dim view of this method of fishing.) "Want to go fishing with us in the morning?" Ken inquired one Friday night before we hit the sack. When I found out what he and his brother had in mind, I declined. I couldn't afford the phone call. But I surely did enjoy eating the 28-pound catfish they brought home before noon that morning.

As you know, years have a way of flying by. Before I could believe it, Ken was out of college, having graduated with top marks on a business degree. With an absolutely gorgeous little wife and with two precious children, he showed up one Sunday morning at our church. I was delighted to see him after so many years and glad to meet his sweet family. He said they probably would be worshiping with our congregation. Of course, I encouraged this and, since I was the main tie they had to us, I went out of my way to make them feel welcome. Ken had a good job handling the insurance concerns of a major corporation in a large local store. Every time I could I stopped by to drink coffee and to renew our friendship. His parents wrote to tell me how pleased they were that Ken and his family were going to church again, evidently for the first time since their marriage. It was an answer to many prayers, they told me.

Then one afternoon, when I stopped by Ken's office to say howdy, he blurted out to me that he was moving. He had resigned his job, he said. His wife was taking the kids and going to her parents' home in Dallas. He was planning to drift toward an older brother's place in Shreveport. "What will you be doing there?" I asked him. He told me he didn't know. That day for the first time I detected a sadness in his eyes, a listlessness in his soul. Signs of spiritual sickness. If he'd been a puppy, I would have felt his nose and taken him to see a vet. Today I look back and wonder if Ken's tragic story might have turned out differently if I had acted on my hunches that day. But I didn't. I stopped by his house to bid him good-bye while they loaded their separated belongings into two trailers. Hers was bulging. His nearly empty. I mentioned the disparity and he shrugged his shoulders. He didn't really care.

Three or four years passed, maybe more, during which time I had almost forgotten Ken existed. Out of sight, out of mind, you know. So I was surprised when his mother called me one day. "Ken's in jail," she wept.

"In jail!?" I exclaimed. She explained, without giving me any details, that he was in a state prison for the criminally insane. I could hardly believe my ears. Ken? The almost perfect son? With the picture-perfect family? With almost unlimited job potential? That Ken? Now imprisoned in a lock-up ward for the mentally ill? It was incredible.

"Please send Ken *The Christian Appeal*," his mother begged me. "Maybe it will help him get his mind straight and make him want to do better." It was the desperate prayer of a heartbroken mother. "Sure," I told her, "I'll be glad to." But, when I heard the rest of the story from some of Ken's relatives, I wondered if we were wasting our postage. His once-brilliant brain was now far too damaged to distinguish love from hate, or good from evil. He was too far gone now to hear the voice of his mother, or his preacher, or his God. Instead he lived in his own private hell of rage and insanity. Jesus told a heartwarming tale about a prodigal son who ran amok in the indulgences of the world for a season and then came back to his senses and returned home penitently to his father's waiting love. Ken Williams never made it home.

He tried to go home, but he waited too long to attempt the journey. For several years, I found out, he had worked at a high-paying airline job his brother finagled for him, but he was at loose ends spiritually. His wife refused to return to him with the kids because she knew what his parents never suspected, that he was addicted to cocaine. She did not intend to raise her children in a home where Daddy spent the rent money on expensive white powder and got so stoned he didn't even know when he abused them. So she vanished quietly, benevolently hoping to spare Ken's mother and father the heartbreak of knowing that their all-American son was a dopehead.

Airlines are not so blind as doting parents. The first time they caught Ken high on the job they suspended him for thirty days and sent him to rehab. The second time, they canned him. Not knowing where else to go, Ken headed home. But, as I said, he had waited too long. Already the circuits of his brain were shorted out, his judgment jammed, by the junk he kept ingesting. When he knocked on the front door of the country house he had grown up in, the wild look in his blood-shot eyes frightened his own mother and made her scream inside, *What is wrong with my baby?*

Far more than she knew. He piddled around the house for a few days, his moods roller-coasting from chattery euphoria to sullen rage. At first his parents tried to make conversation. Soon they just tiptoed around this frightening stranger, trying futilely not to trigger one his demented dialogues or an explosion of his wrath. Ken's father hid the family guns. Alone in their bedroom his terrified parents whispered plans for taking him to the state hospital in Fort Smith or Little Rock for psychiatric care, but neither of them dared to discuss such an option with Ken. So the bad situation quickly got worse. With all their hearts they wanted to love the prodigal who finally had found his way home, but by now he was beyond love.

Either drunk or drugged — they never knew which for sure — Ken decided late one evening to pay a visit to his high school sweetheart down in the village. His messed-up mind either did not recall or did not care that she had now been married for several years. To an oil-field roughneck. A huge, muscular man. Realizing that Ken was intoxicated, the lady's husband tried at first to coax him to go home and leave them alone, but Ken had one intent in his muddled mind. He persisted in his romantic overtures to the man's wife, becoming increasingly angry and lewd. At some point in this bad scene Ken went too far. Too far for any red-blooded husband to tolerate peaceably. The enraged man knocked Ken down, battering him and kicking him. Ken survived the attack only because neighbors finally teamed up to restrain the enraged husband, whose steel-toed work boots by then had made mush of Ken's face and head.

For weeks Ken lay in intensive care near death. Nobody thought he would survive. It would have been a blessing, most agree, if he had not, because the Ken who left that hospital was less than human. The part of the brain that made Ken to be Ken was dead. He had been lobotomized by a work boot. Right and wrong no longer registered in his scrambled cranium. In such a condition it was inevitable that the animal part of Ken, still very much alive in him, would dictate his behavior. It was only a matter of time until an innocent victim fell prey to his inhuman instincts. The jury deliberated Ken's fate while his own mother prayed fervently to God that they would lock up her son where he could never do that to any woman again.

Several years after Ken was sentenced to confinement in the state maximum security prison for the criminally insane, his father died while working at the family sawmill one day. Notified of the death, the prison chaplain made his way to Ken's cell. When he told him his father was dead, Ken smiled faintly, as if the chaplain had delivered an insignificant piece of news about a total stranger, and then returned to his game of solitaire without a flicker of grief.

Every year or so state law requires the parole board to consider releasing Ken from prison. Every year or so Ken's mother and all of us who know him well pray for the sanity of that board, which has a well-documented reputation for turning vicious criminals loose to prowl again. Ken Williams is where he needs to be. What is broken in his brain cannot be fixed. It will be nothing short of a tragedy if this prodigal ever comes home again.

In the light of this story, can you see why the Scriptures warn us so urgently: *"Today, when you hear His voice, do not harden your hearts."*

Today you can still hear God. But if you tune Him out, the wisdom and warnings in His word will become fainter and fainter until they no longer touch your heart and penetrate your soul.

Today your conscience is still tender enough to sound guilt-warnings when you stray from purity and dabble with sin. But his Holy Spirit will not struggle with you forever, the Bible warns. If you persist in sin, one day he will withdraw and leave you to be destroyed by whatever evil you have chosen.

My urgent task is to be sure that you hear His voice *while you still can.* To call you to receive His mercy and imitate His holiness while you are still able to hear Him.

I knew Ken Williams well enough to know that he never really meant to turn his back on God. Not permanently, at least. Not forever. Maybe for a few years while he was in college. After all, with parents as religious as his were, he needed a breather. And the early years of marriage were not an easy time to concentrate on God. Going to church and studying the Bible are hard to fit into a young couple's leisure schedule, especially when you marry somebody who thinks church-going is something you do at weddings and funerals. But, in Ken's mind, these were only temporary stages in his life. A little vacation from the rigors of religion while he got his family started and got his job on track. Soon he would get back to his faith. Back to his raising. Back to the God of his mother and father. He just needed a little more time . . . .

But somewhere along this lengthy line of rationalization, on a day when Ken probably didn't even know it, he turned his back on God one time too many and his once-tender heart was forever hardened.

Don't let that happen to you. *"Today, while you hear His voice —"* is the time to get serious again about your religion.

"Today, while you hear His voice —" is the time to rearrange your priorities and put God first on your calendar, in your checkbook, in all your commitments.

"Today, while you hear His voice —" reach out for His grace. Accept His Son. Proudly wear His name.

When Hope Vanishes

"The steadfast love of the LORD never ceases, his mercies never come to an end; they are new every morning; great is thy faithfulness" (Lamentations 3:22-23).

Some things, once they are broken, can never be fixed.

A cracked porcelain china cup.

A pulley bone that has been pulled.

A diamond that shatters when it's being cut.

No glue on earth is super enough, no hand skillful enough to mend such things. Some of the pieces are always missing. Even the most delicate efforts to repair the damage leaves permanent scars.

So it is with our attempts to repair the human psyche. The mind once fragmented by schizophrenic furies never seems to be completely whole again. Even the wisest therapies and the latest drugs seem at best to produce only a temporary patch, a momentary mask for the madness that lurks in the soul, just waiting for a chance to break loose again. Wholeness for such people seems to be an elusive goal, desperately sought but seldom realized.

If someone you love has suffered serious mental illness, you understand what I'm saying. But, if by God's grace you have avoided this devastation, let me explain it by telling you the story of a lady I will call Samantha Cole. A few of the places and times in the tale I have altered to hide the true identity of Samantha and her family, but the story I'm going to tell you is true and the horrors I will describe are painfully, tragically real.

"I put Samantha in the hospital yesterday," her godly father told me through tears one morning.

"Really?" I inquired. Samantha had been home less than two weeks after the birth of her first child, so I jumped to an obvious but wrong conclusion. "Is she having troubles after the birth?" I guessed.

"Well, yes, and no," he hesitated, trying to control his emotions. "I guess the troubles are related to the birth in some way. The doctors seem to think so. Yesterday she threatened to kill the baby and then tried to take her own life."

Gentle Jim Cole could have slugged me in the gut and not hit me any harder than he did with that piece of news. Samantha? Lovely, quiet, smiling Samantha who had grown up on a church pew with hardly a hint of the upheavals that sometimes unsettle teenagers? This Samantha had tried to kill herself and her baby? I couldn't believe it.

Tears rolled down Jim's cheeks as he unfolded the incredible details of the day just past. Early that morning Samantha's young husband had called his in-laws.

Normally timid Samantha had erupted like a volcano spewing profanity and angry threats on everybody in sight. Her hapless husband had tried for hours to get her under control, but nothing seemed to work. At his wit's end, he summoned Samantha's parents, who were equally baffled by their daughter's sudden transformation into a wild woman. Through their long-time family doctor they finally got an appointment for Samantha with a psychiatrist. With his help, Jim Cole told me, they had committed Samantha to a nearby psychiatric hospital, both for her own safety and to try to find out why she had gone berserk.

As he looked back at this time years later, Jim Cole said the days that followed Samantha's first commitment were the nearest thing to hell he had ever known on this earth. He and his family were hurt and bewildered when the psychiatrist refused to let any of them visit Samantha during the first days of treatment. Having never been around a schizophrenic person before, this good family had no way to know that Samantha's irrational, obsessive anger would focus on the people nearest to her. Coming to comfort and love her, they actually, by their very presence, would enrage her and undo all the counselors and doctors were trying to do to restore calm and order to her chaotic mind.

Over a month passed before Samantha was allowed brief visits to family and friends outside the hospital. When she came home on a pass, the family made sure she was never alone with her baby. The doctor had warned them that he could not predict how she might react to the infant who had triggered her initial break. Watching her as unobtrusively as they could to assure the baby's safety, family members were relieved to see no indication that she might harm the child. At the same time, however, they were distressed to see that Samantha apparently had not one ounce of affection or attraction toward her little one. She was like a zombie, like a lifeless puppet with wooden arms and a painted-on face. Not once did she smile or coo in response to her baby's giggles and gurgles. Whatever normally prompts a mother's love was dormant or dead in Samantha, lost somewhere deep within her. Her grieving family watched these heartbreaking scenes and knew it might be months, maybe even years, before she could be a mother to her little boy.

Nobody can ever know how hard Samantha's young husband struggled to make their ill-fated marriage work. Wed to an empty shell of a woman so loaded with medication and so damaged by electro-shock therapy that she had forgotten how to laugh or smile or make the small talk essential to daily family fun, the poor man floundered. No human being is prepared to deal with what Samantha put him through. The adjustments of early marriage years are tough enough when both mates are able to think clearly and react maturely. When one partner has been reduced to a hardly functioning emotional vegetable, the marriage's chances are nil indeed. Before the year was done Samantha had moved back into her parents' less-than-adequate home along with the baby she could not care for. Thus the disaster of her mental illness blighted both homes, decimating her own and dooming her parents to live out what should have been their good years in the upheaval and uncertainty of recurring insanity. For more than two decades now these good people have had no good years.

A big part of the tragedy in this situation is the lack

of any light at the end of the tunnel. In a culture that expects science or medicine to pull a magic rabbit out of the hat to solve any problem, the Cole family finds themselves enmeshed in a mess that has no medical solution. In a church fellowship that speaks glibly of answers to faithful prayer, the Coles' most fervent prayers and their most loving efforts seem to have no effectiveness in lessening Samantha's affliction. For every good month, Samantha has ten that are nothing short of hellish. Hospitalization follows bleak hospitalization, with more shock treatments that temporarily zap her obsessive fears but also erase much of the mental data necessary for normal living. Nothing really seems to help much. And therein lies the greatest pain for Samantha and her family — the absence of any hope that things will ever be much better.

How can a person survive without hope? When they must plaintively cry with Job on the ash-heap, "Who can see any hope for me?" (17:15, NIV). We bravely face the surgeon's knife when he can promise healing and health after the pain. We endure the rigors of a seemingly endless educational regimen when we can envision the better job and the broader opportunities for service the hard-won degree will make possible. "Weeping may tarry for the night, but joy comes with the morning," the holy Scriptures assure us. That's the normal pattern. Temporary troubles followed by renewed well-being. Anybody can make it through the night. Even the blackest of nights. But what do you do when the night lasts forever? "Yet when I hoped for good," Job said, "evil came; when I looked for light, then came darkness." Like the Coles he lamented, "The churning inside me never stops; days of suffering confront me" (30:26-27, NIV).

Fellow-Strugglers

If you find yourself snared in a no-win situation like this, let me share with you the experience of one person who learned to cope with the loss of normal hope. Though it may be meager help at best, perhaps it will at least help us some when we find ourselves caught in unending miseries to know that we are not the only ones who have been sucked into a black hole of endless woe. Countless men and women of God have known this fate. One such person was the great prophet Jeremiah. Hear his lamentation as he wails,

> He has driven me and brought me
>> into darkness without any light;
> surely against me he turns his hand
>> again and again the whole day long.
> He has made my flesh and my skin waste away
>> and broken my bones;
> he has besieged and enveloped me
>> with bitterness and tribulation;
> he has made me dwell in darkness
>> like the dead of long ago.
> He has walled me about so that I cannot escape;
>> he has put heavy chains on me;
> though I call and cry for help,
>> he shuts out my prayer;
> he has blocked my ways with hewn stones,
>> he has made my paths crooked.
> He is to me like a bear lying in wait,
>> like a lion in hiding;
> he led me off my way and tore me to pieces;
>> he has made me desolate;
> he bent his bow
>> and set me as a mark for his arrow.
> He drove into my heart
>> the arrows of his quiver. . . .
>>> . . . He has made me cower in ashes;

my soul is bereft of peace;
    I have forgotten what happiness is.
So I say, "Gone is my glory
    and my expectation from the Lord."
Remember my affliction and my bitterness,
    the wormwood and the gall!
My soul continually thinks of it,
and is bowed down within me.

(Lamentations 3:2-20)

Have you been there, too? Is Jeremiah describing you? If so, does it help in our own inescapable anguish to know that words like these were written by one of God's most faithful followers? Does it help to know, as the apostle Peter pointed out to some of his converts, that "the same experience of suffering is required of your brotherhood throughout the world"? That trouble has not been reserved for you alone?

It may also help to know that although Jeremiah lost all visible, physical reasons to hope, he got through that hard time by focusing his faith on the God who had always loved him and always would. "But this I call to mind," Jeremiah prayed in his darkest moment, "and therefore I have hope:"

The steadfast love of the LORD never ceases,
    his mercies never come to an end;
they are new every morning;
    great is thy faithfulness.
"The Lord is my portion," says my soul,
    therefore I will hope in him."
The Lord is good to those who wait for him,
    to the soul that seeks him;
it is good that one should wait quietly
    for the salvation of the LORD.

(Lamentations 3:21-26)

Do you have that kind of faith? Are you convinced, as Jeremiah was, of God's unfailing goodness? When the clouds stay dark and low and refuse to go away, do you still believe that somewhere beyond them the sun still shines with all its brilliance and warmth? If in the depths of your most depressing difficulties you can still say with the Psalmist, "O give thanks to the Lord, for he is good," then your soul is protected from the bitterness and despair that threaten to undo us when troubles seem harder and longer than we can bear.

Jim Cole knew this. Long before Samantha's interminable bout with mental illness came to haunt his good family, Jim placed his faith in a God whose goodness outlasts and overcomes any evil Satan may inflict upon us. So when troubles came, Jim was prepared. He knew where to find strength when strength fails, where to find hope when hope vanishes. He knew that only in the Eternal God, who proved his limitless love to us on Calvary, can we find light when darkness engulfs our souls. With the ancient Psalmist, Jim could pray,

> For God alone my soul waits in silence;
> > from him comes my salvation.
> He only is my rock and my salvation;
> > my fortress, I shall not be greatly moved . . . .
> For God alone my soul waits in silence,
> > for my hope is from him.
> He only is my rock and my salvation;
> > my fortress; I shall not be shaken.
> On God rests my deliverance and my honor;
> > my mighty rock, my refuge is God.
> Trust in him at all times, O people;
> > pour out your heart before him,
> > God is a refuge for us.
> > > (Psalm 62:1-2, 5-8)

When Samantha's troubles broke his heart and almost broke his spirit, Jim Cole proved the truth of Isaiah's precious promise:

> But they who wait for the LORD
>   shall renew their strength;
> They shall mount up with wings like eagles,
>   they shall run and not be weary,
>   they shall walk and not faint (Isa. 40:31).

To those whose suffering has been harsh and long, the Scriptures admonish, "Let us hold fast the confession of our hope without wavering." Why? Because "he who promised is faithful" (Hebrews 10:23). This is our only hope: not our own strength, but the faithfulness and strength of the One who promises to sustain us. To those who are enduring hardship, the apostle Paul writes, "Rejoice in your hope, be patient in tribulation, be constant in prayer" (Romans 12:12). The alternative, of course, is to give up. To surrender to our anger and self-pity and frustration.

If you are near to this kind of despair today, let me join Paul in praying for you, "May the God of hope fill you with all joy and peace in believing, so that by the power of the Holy Spirit you may abound in hope" (Romans 15:13). And along with that prayer I would admonish you: Trust in the Lord. Instead of focusing on your trials, concentrate on his unfailing goodness, so that you can say with Job, "Though he slay me, yet will I hope in him" (13:15, NIV).

Christianity Without Easter

"If for this life only we have hope . . . , we are of all men most miserable"
(1 Corinthians 15:19).

Can you imagine what it would be like to have Christianity without Easter?

> Some of us can. We grew up in a fellowship which
> carefully avoided observing any religious holidays.
> We usually celebrated Christmas in our churches by
> preaching surly sermons entitled "Why We Don't
> Believe in Christmas."
> And Easter came and went without a lily.
> > Certainly with no sunrise service.
> > And as nearly as possible without any mention of
> > the resurrection.
> We had Christianity without Easter.

But that's not what I'm talking about. Can you imagine the Christian faith
  — without the stone rolled away?
  — without the excitement of the angel's message?
  — without the incredible hope of the empty tomb?

Can you imagine what Christianity would be like
  — without the joy of knowing Jesus and the power of
    His resurrection?
  — without the promise of new life now?
  — without the assurance that we will still live after
    this life?
    Christianity without Easter would be
    like a girl without a smile,
        like a rose without a smell,
            like a year without spring.

Without Easter, for example what would have happened to Emory Sullivan?
    Emory was a raw-boned, rough-talking galoot who tried to act like he was straight off the farm while he assembled hi-tech components in an aerospace plant.
        The country-boy image he tried so hard to project clashed with the competence he displayed on the job.
            Almost as much as his overt behavior clashed with his true nature the first time he met me.
If it had been left up to Emory Sullivan, he would just as soon to have never met me.
    He had spent his thirty years avoiding religion and churches and preachers — quite effectively.
    Preachers bothered Emory, so he did his best to keep them at a distance.

He knew how.
The first sentence Emory ever spoke to me consisted of three expletives (not deleted) and at least four obscenities.

"Hello, Emory," I greeted him and told him who I was. "Your friend Blanche asked me to stop by the hospital to look in on you," I explained.
Instantly the air turned blue.

He was not attacking me.

He was not angry or belligerent.

He *was* very profane, and his profanity served one purpose: it made sure that this preacher did not get too close.
But I needed to get close. Emory and his family needed me — or somebody like me — to get close, because their world was just about to come apart.

They were going to need all the loving and all the faith they could get.

Ellen was their firstborn.

Rambunctious.

Honey-haired.

Always smiling.

Ellen was the delight of their eyes, the spice of their days, the joy of their life.

How could her daddy face the fact that his precious Ellen, who was now four, would likely never be any more?

Ellen beamed up at me from her hospital bed. She was truly a radiant child, and she was not the least bit inhibited by the fact that I was a stranger she had never seen before.

As for me, it was love at first sight.
Ellen's mother was embarrassed by her husband's outbursts of profanity. She tried to cover the awkwardness and fill the silence by telling me what I already knew — that Ellen only a few weeks before had begun to drag one toe, and then to stumble.

Emory punctuated her tale with his profanity. But I saw beyond his risqué remarks and raw metaphors.

In the words and in the eyes of those shell-shocked parents I read their hurt. I saw their pain.

All this was happening in the days when brain surgery was almost unheard of. "The doctors say they just managed to cut a tumor like Ellen's out of a monkey's brain," Emory inserted. Trying, I think, to convince himself to hope. "The blankety-blank monkey could still walk and go the bathroom when they got through whittlin' on him, too!"

Tomorrow they would "whittle" on Ellen.
Dear Ellen.
Blonde-headed.
Happy-eyed.
Always smiling.
Dear little Ellen.
When her daddy found out that he couldn't wilt my ears or sear my soul with his vocabulary, with all his terrified heart he welcomed my prayers for his child.

Seven hours the surgery lasted that next day.
Weary doctors without smiles appeared then to tell us, "We took out as much of the tumor as we dared. In fact, we may have cut in deeper than we should

have. We do not know if Ellen will be able to speak or to move or to see when she wakes up. We're sorry to tell you that the part of the tumor we did remove was definitely malignant."

Imagine the relief, the unbelief, when two hours later Ellen opened her eyes, and smiled, and said, "Hi, Daddy." And then, like most four-year-olds, said, "I'm hungry."

A second surgery had to follow soon after the first, to relieve the pressure of her swelling brain.

Then recovery seemed like magic.

Ellen looked at first like a miniature mummy, her little girl's head swathed in a turban of gauze and two-inch tape and cotton padding.

But the day came when she smiled an impish grin at me and lifted her top-knot of bandages to reveal peach-fuzz blonde hair growing all over her head.

Something else was growing, too. An unlikely friend-ship.

Between Emory and me.

He still checked me out with occasional spurts of sailor-talk, just to see if I actually accepted him as he was and liked him in spite of it.

By now I knew that Emory was an O.K. guy. The Lord still had lots of work to do on Emory, but He did on me as well.

And I knew now that Emory — to his own amaze-ment — liked me, too.

During the months that followed, when the Sullivans came into town for Ellen's check-ups, they brought their younger children to our home. Nita and I babysat so that both parents could be present during the long examinations.

"Guess what I did yesterday?" Ellen grinned at us on one of those visits.

By now her honey-blonde hair was Buster Browned almost at normal length and Ellen looked like health personified.

"I won the foot-race for five-year-olds at the Buckeye fair!" she announced with her eyes just dancing. From Emory's proud-papa look you would have thought she'd won the Olympics.

Early that fall our telephone rang.

"We thought you would want to know," Ellen's mother told us. "Ellen goes back into the hospital tomorrow."

As the summer had waned, they told us later, so had Ellen's strength.

Then she had begun once more to stumble.

Hope was gone. Fear froze their faces when we joined them one more time in that familiar hospital corridor.

Without surgery Ellen had no hope, the doctors had told them.

With surgery she really had none, they might also have said. But Emory knew it without the telling.

From that final operation little Ellen never woke up. For several days she lay in her bed not moving.

Dear Ellen,
    Dimpled cheeks now hollow,
        Head shaved,
            A tube in her nose,
                Dear little Ellen,
            Wrapped in bandages like grave clothes.

We gathered in a little country church. (Emory really was a country boy after all.)

　We came there that morning — a diverse host of working associates and neighbors and friends and nurses who had fallen in love with that irrepressible child.

　From Emory's farm country and from the busy city nearby we came to that rustic church
　　— drawn there by a brave little girl who had taught all of us to defy death.
　We came there to weep with her family — and to affirm with them what Emory probably could not have affirmed a year before — that, although death had come, death had not won.

Now I ask you, how much good would my Christianity have been to Emory Sullivan — without Easter?

　"If Christ has not been raised," the apostle Paul concluded, "then our preaching is in vain, and your faith is in vain."
　The whole thing is an empty shell — a cruel sham — without Easter.

If Jesus has been dead for almost 2,000 years,
　why should I turn the other cheek
　　or go the second mile?
　Why should I pray for those who persecute me
　　and bless my enemies
　　　— if His Enemy was able to put Him permanently in a grave?
　　　— if His life could be ended with a spear and three nails?

It would be hard to conceive of any concept less compelling,
     less worthy of devotion, less helpful in distress, than
          Christianity without Easter.

"But in fact," Paul exulted, "Christ *has* been raised, the first-fruits of those who have fallen asleep."
     And we gather, along with millions of believers around the world each Easter, to celebrate the hope that rises from that most important of all historical events.

Someone has said that "the secret of life is hope."
     We find that hope in the resurrection of our Lord.
     We find that hope in Easter.